The Marathons of Life

By

Bob "Bart" Bardwell

Bob and Jode Bardwell
7291 CR 6 SW
Stewartville, Minnesota 55976

(507) 533-9516
Toll free 1-888-598-4300

Printed and bound in the U.S.A.

Bardwell, Bob "Bart"

The Marathons of Life
ISBN 0-9658759-0-3

Inspirational/Autobiography

The Marathons of Life

By

Bob "Bart" Bardwell

2015

Nels
Dont Quit
Finish Strong!
BBB

ACKNOWLEDGMENTS

I am grateful for the support and encouragement given to me by so many people.

Thank you - Gary Froiland! Gary has done all the graphic art work, design of the front and back cover, all pencil drawings, as well as layout of prints and pictures. I would describe my stories to Gary and he would make them come to life on paper.

Gary lives in Stewartville, Minnesota with his wife, Elaine, and Joshua age 10 and Jessica age 7. Besides being an artist, Gary is a musician. They have a band called, "The Froiland Bluegrass Band."

Thank you - Victor Lee! I became acquainted with Victor through his written articles in "Sports Spectrum" magazine. I caught up with Victor after the Paralympics in Atlanta in August 1996. Victor has taken my 'rough draft' and turned it into a book. Thank you Victor for your editing, suggesting, patience and believing in my story. Victor lives in Wake Forest, NC with his wife Judy and daughter Jessica.

Contributing editors, special helps, and encouragers:

Susan J. Benson
Randy Miller
Jenny Nelson
Cynndra Regehr
MaryAnn Schultz
Roger Sinning

FORWARD

As far back as 1980 several friends encouraged me to write a book about my journey. I thought that was a good idea, but did not feel like the time was right. Seventeen years later I turned this idea into a reality. However, it was a marathon (challenge) in itself with the delays, changes, lack of funds, discouragements, not so friendly computer problems, and perseverance needed.

There was a time when I questioned if I would make the first category of three types of people 1) those who make it happen, and 2) those who plan to make it happen, and 3) those who wonder what happened.

I have experienced plenty of athletic successes as you will read about, but I wasn't then nor am I today the greatest athlete. I have never set any world records, or won first place in the Boston Marathon. Rather, I think my story is one of accomplishment, hard work and vision.

My journey is a living witness to the "love and grace" of God. Leaving God out of my life would be like a carpenter trying to build a house without a hammer. I believe in giving credit where credit is due. God gave me my life and I'm breathing His air, why not credit him for turning my 'tragedies into triumphs'? No, I can't convert the world, nor is that my task. Rather, through sharing with you my journey you can see as the song says, "How Great Thou Art".

I am writing this book in an effort to *make a difference in your life* regardless of what marathon you are facing today.

Your friend,

Bob

DEDICATION

I dedicate this book to my wife, Jode. It would not be a reality without her involvement, suggestions, encouragement and late nights, not to mention her editing out old girlfriends, etc. Jode, I love you. Thank you for being an inspirational part of my life. God gave me a wonderful gift when He gave me you and our children.

TABLE OF CONTENTS

1

CATERPILLAR CRUNCH

Black smoke billowed into the blue sky from the diesel engine of the Caterpillar machine I was operating. The day of my accident I was working on shaping and landscaping the high school track in Plainview, Minnesota. I was hauling several hundred yards of dirt with a Cat and scraper. The machine I was operating was a Caterpillar D7G and the scraper I was pulling was a large rubber tire machine. I was pulling on the lever of the winch, preparing to dump my last load of dirt before breaking for lunch. Just at that moment a half-inch steel cable snapped, and I, in disgust, stopped the machine, jumped to the ground, and scrambled beneath the bucket to repair the severed cable.

site of the accident

It was high noon, July 16, 1973, and my life was about to change forever.

I had never had a broken bone. My only previous hospital visits were to have my appendix removed in the seventh grade and my tongue sewn back on after getting an elbow in the chops during a district wrestling match in my junior year in high school.

I had worked for my father's construction company for seven years and had learned to operate the largest earth moving equipment in the world. Operating large Caterpillar equipment takes constant awareness of the dangers involved. Besides being taught the importance of safety, I was also aware of the necessity for regular, daily maintenance.

Frustrated, sweaty, and ready for lunch, I got down beside the scraper to thread in a new half-inch cable so I could dump the load. I was sitting on the ground with some large tools when one of my fellow workers got up on the Cat and accidentally pushed a lever the wrong way, instantly dropping the scraper — *loaded with approximately twenty tons of dirt.*

I had just completed a ten-year wrestling career, so I could have maybe lifted ten tons *(just kidding!)* but twenty tons was too much of a match. When it fell, I was instantly unconscious and unable to breathe, having my shoulders smashed down to my knees. My lower back was crushed, damaging my spinal cord. My lungs were collapsed and several ribs broken. (Now if you have a choice which bone in your body to break, I *strongly recommend* not choosing the backbone!)

My fellow worker saw me and tried to raise the scraper bucket, but to no avail. When it dropped, the cable had gotten snarled so that it would not raise. With the help of a shovel to loosen the dirt below me and some strong tugging, several co-workers got me out and laid me flat and I soon regained consciousness. The city emergency whistle blew, and within minutes the ambulance arrived.

I was in a state of shock from the trauma, but was completely conscious during the half-hour ride to St. Mary's Hospital, which is a part of the world-famous Mayo Clinic in Rochester, Minnesota. I well remember the physical agony and seemingly eternal wait to get several x-rays before any pain relievers were given to me. My parents were vacationing in northern Minnesota in the Bemidji area near my relatives. Eventually, a policeman tracked them down and told them the news.

With only a sketchy report of my injury, they had a long and anxious drive to Rochester.

When they arrived, I was in the midst of seven hours of surgery. Two seven-inch long Harrington rods were placed alongside my spine and bone was taken from my hip to fuse the spine and rods together. I was in the Intensive Care Unit for the next seven days. Because of the trauma, I could not use my arms for about three or four days, so when I regained consciousness, I felt like I was paralyzed from the neck down. When family was allowed to see me, the one thing I wanted them to do was to move and exercise my arms.

Although I did not have a body cast, for four weeks I was put in a foster frame, a sandwich-like bed, with me as the butter. Believe me, the bread was not like fresh, homemade, wheat brand, but rather week-old hard toast. The top and bottom between which I was sandwiched were made of canvas with metal on the sides. Because I was not to move my back for the next four weeks this contraption allowed me to be rotated to:

(1) prevent pressure sores,
(2) protect the ceiling from holes from my long hours of staring, and
(3) entertain the nurses and friends, who seemed to love turning the crank and making the room a kaleidoscope for me.

Word of my injury quickly spread and soon flowers, letters, cards, phone calls and visitors began coming, mercifully occupying some of the endless days. Soon I was placed on the rehabilitation floor.

My doctor, Robert Sawtell, was a very kind, honest and encouraging doctor, yet straight-forward in his assessment of my situation.

His prognosis:

— Hospitalized for six months.
— Never to walk again (T-12 paraplegic).
— Could not father a child.
— A complete new lifestyle.

Among the first steps after I was able to sit up, was getting a back brace; physical and occupational therapy followed. Frustration was always alongside. One of the exercises during physical therapy was to strap on my long leg braces and stand up between two parallel bars. When I stood I felt like the giant Goliath.

Once when standing, the phone rang and the therapist asked if I could stand by myself while he answered it. Determined as I have always been, I said yes. He hadn't been gone long when I lost my balance and fell to the floor. With knees that wouldn't bend, it was a long fall! I had to get X-rays, but did not have any additional injury. One of my lasting images from that time is of the nurse who rolled into my room with an Everest and Jennings wheelchair with shiny stainless steel and green fabric.

Across the back of the chair was a wide piece of masking tape. Written on it: *Bob Bardwell*. The reality hit me hard for the first time that *this injury might be permanent.*

Up until then I was in bed or a hospital chair and had only seen others in wheelchairs. Reality slapped me hard again when I sat up for the first time. Sitting up and not having any feeling from the waist down was a new and very unusual feeling — there's nothing like it, believe me! I felt like I was being suspended in the air, touching nothing and having no balance, not to mention feeling dizzy and queasy because I hadn't been in a vertical position for about a month.

When I sat up I was able to see my legs for the first time. The legs that had always taken me wherever I wanted to go, that had the spring to do round-offs and the strength to support a winning wrestler, had atrophied so severe that they were about half their normal size. I was both shocked and discouraged as I gazed at my skinny and useless legs, remembering what they had been just a short while ago.

The reality of my situation has always brought certain frustrations. Striving toward more autonomy after rehabilitation, I was eager to get some hand controls installed in my Chevrolet El Camino. I had very little practice using my sliding board in order to transfer out of my wheelchair into my car. Inching along the board, I was able to make it to the car seat. Driving a car without legs to step on the brakes or give it some gas was a strange adjustment. The hands have to do it all! I highly recommend learning to drive in the country, rather than downtown. It gets a bit confusing, and believe me cows are a bit more friendly to honk at than people late for work!

As the prognosis sank in, the future faded away. Questions filled my head and heart.

Why me?
What did I do to deserve this?
Where was God when I needed Him most?
Who says I won't walk again!?

Anger toward the co-worker who dropped the bucket crept into my head. And I wondered, *"What in the world can you do that's positive in a wheelchair besides blend in at the health care center for the elderly?"*

I realize now that some questions never get directly answered, but time has a way of making sense of others.

Of all the gifts given me, one sits outside my office door. A friend from Minneapolis named Glen brought in this very heavy box, in which I found a rock. The rock has a symbolic purpose, as on it is written: *"And we know that in all things God works for the good of those who love Him..."* — Romans 8:28

Could this be part of His plan? I had known this promise for many years but now had to put it to the test and see if God stood behind it. Believing that God is too WISE to make mistakes, and too LOVING to be unkind, spared me the destructive path of bitterness, anger, and denial. During my hard time of recovery, the encouragement that visitors gave me was invaluable. The first person using a wheelchair to stop by for a visit was Glen White, who was paralyzed from the waist down in an automobile accident. Glen remains one of my encouragers. The time he took to stop in and share his story, and then to see his life blossom was, and is, mind boggling. He was one of the people who helped me realize there was still purpose to my life. Another great encouragement to me was the entire wedding party of brother- and sister-in-law, Joel and Carol Raygor, who came to visit. In such circumstances, it's important that a patient not be made to feel isolated from friends, family and the rest of the world.

Being human and having an injury to this extent brings normal thoughts of bitterness and resentment. *But you do not have to allow them to control or destroy your future.* You must deal with them, and move on.

"Pain is inevitable, but misery is optional."
*Tim Hansel

I have contemplated this thought many times in the years since the accident. I remember being dismissed from the supportive environment of the hospital, and going back home to face the stark reality of my future: never being able to walk again.

*Used with permission.

2

NORTHWOODS OF MINNESOTA

Being raised in northern Minnesota is like growing up in an outdoor Paradise.

Besides all the farm animals, we had lots of deer, rabbits, wolves, bear, and plenty of fish in the fresh lakes and streams. I was born May 25, 1947 in the small town of Fosston, Minnesota about 150 miles north of Lake Wobegan. I have an older brother and sister and a younger sister and two younger brothers. My parents are Lester and Jeanne Bardwell. We lived on a farm not far from Fosston, near a small town called Clearbrook.

My dad was born and raised near Clearbrook, on a farm along the Clearwater River. Can you imagine living today along a river that is clear? At that time it was clean enough to drink from. I walked with my brothers and sisters about two miles to a country school each day. My first grade teacher was Edith Holty. My aunt, Bernice Berg, was the teacher for the older students. Each row of desks was a grade, going up through the eighth grade. I know this sounds like scenes out of the old West, but life really was that rural, and that simple, in 1953.

I recall three of us first graders. My cousin, Dan Berg, a neighbor girl, and myself. As first graders, we were favored by getting out for lunch break and recess first. I have three memories of recess, 1) building forts out of sumac and hiding from the older students and 2) taking old gears off machinery, sticking a broom handle in the center and making roads and 3) build-

ing forts inside the large snow drifts.

I also remember walking to school in the cold winter and my sister, Kathy, lost her boot in the snow bank and we had to walk about one-half mile to the closest neighbor to get help.

After first grade the country school closed down and we were all bussed to the elementary school in Clearbrook. Sometime during my third-grade year we moved to Pasadena, California, where my maternal grandparents lived. My dad had met mom while in the Navy in southern California.

My dad had a small airplane and would go hunting for fox from the air. At that time, they could shoot them right out of the plane. During the first ten years of living in the northwoods of Minnesota, I developed a real love for all of God's creation. I was definitely an outdoors kid.

Another important part of my upbringing was going to Sunday School and Summer Bible School. We attended a country church called Clover Bible Chapel. I remember walking several miles to summer Bible schools, attending large evangelistic tent meetings, and having family devotions and Bible memory. Dad often told us about when he was younger and would describe how he and his two brothers would be upstairs all in one bed, covered up with several blankets during the winter months, looking up through the cracks in the ceiling and watching the stars. Downstairs, they would hear their mom and dad praying aloud for each one of their children by name. Dad reminds us how richly blessed we are today to have Godly grandparents.

> I credit many of the blessings of God on my life today to the prayers of my parents and grandparents.

Today I enjoy going back to northern Minnesota to see the old homestead and visit my aunts, uncles and cousins. Some of my cousins grow several hundred acres of wild rice and vegetables, while others are farmers and lumberjacks. I have gone on several good hunting and fishing trips to northern Minnesota as well. It remains a warm, special place in my heart, a place that shaped much of the love I have today for the outdoors.

COLORADO MOUNTAIN STREAM

A Bag of Tools

Isn't it strange that princes and kings
and clowns with capers in sawdust rings,
and common folks like you and me
are builders for eternity.

To each is given a bag of tools
a shapeless mass and a book of rules,
and each must make err life is flown
a stumbling block or a stepping stone.

—R. L. Sharpe

Good parenting requires selflessness. I'm very thankful that my father understood that.

Dad always needed me to work summers for his construction company. I didn't ever consider anything else — until the summer after my freshman year of college.

Chuck Woods, of Houston, Texas, was my roommate my freshmen year. He had worked at a camp in Colorado the previous summer. The camp was called Horn Creek Ranch, and was started and operated by Paul and Jean Zeller. It was an independent evangelical Christian camp in Westcliffe, Colorado (about 90 miles southwest of Colorado Springs). Throughout the year, Chuck told me of his wonderful adventures and experiences at Horn Creek. It sounded great, but I knew I was headed back to the Caterpillar.

On June 1, the phone rang. "Hey Bart, this is Chuck at Horn Creek. Paul told me to call you and ask if you might be able to come to Horn Creek and work for the summer."

"Why? What's going on, and what would I do?" I questioned.

"They need a wrangler to take trail rides in the mountains," Chuck said.

"I'll talk to dad about it and get back to you soon," I answered with excitement.

Though dad was counting on me, he saw what an opportunity I had and unselfishly said "Yes". That is a great testimony to my dad's character.

Within a few days I was at Horn Creek. I realized later that working with horses was a nice lure to come to the camp. I did a lot with the horses, but I also cleaned toilets, did dishes, cleaned cabins, did lawn work, and had counseling opportunities. (I use the same luring techniques, now that I have my own camp!)

It was an exciting and incredible summer for me. I met kids from all over the country. Weekly I would take a group of six to twelve people backpacking on horseback in the mountains along Rainbow Trail.

Chuck, the camp cook who played banjo and several other instruments professionally, put together a singing group called the Horn Creek Mountain Men. I played the tub (a wash tub, broom handle, and four-foot piece of clothes line string) and Chuck taught me to play the ukulele.

Other jobs at camp included fixing fences, climbing Horn Mountain, sharing at Friday night campfires, and helping Chuck in the kitchen.

I also found out that the most beautiful girls in the world came to Horn Creek. One that I took for several trail rides was a Southern Belle from Texas. She had come up for one week of camp with a group, and showed up at the stables the first day for a ride.

The old trail ride joke came in handy: You're out on the trail with the group and finally you ditch them. You and your chick ride off and come to a stream. You get off the horses and let them have some water. One horse nudges another, acts romantic, rubs its nose and moves a little closer. "I'd kinda' like to do that," you say to your girl.

"Go ahead," she says. "It's your horse."

When she left, I thought I wouldn't survive. We kept in touch through the mail for a few years, but I didn't see her, and our postal romance ended.

One of the greatest benefits of the summer proved to be my own heart searching. Listening to the speakers and programs each week had a big influence on my life. Every week we were challenged to put Jesus Christ first in our lives, and live the abundant life He had to offer. About mid-summer, early in the morning before breakfast, I had gone out and sat down beside the cool mountain stream called Horn Creek. I did a lot of soul searching that morning.

> I looked up behind me and saw majestic Horn
> Mountain, and out in front about forty miles of
> the beautiful valley, and realized how small I
> was and how big God is.

I had made commitments to God before and had a relationship with Jesus Christ as my personal Savior. However, sitting along Horn Creek that morning, that relationship took on a new meaning. I rededicated my life and determined to follow Him daily. I told God that whatever He wanted to do with my life, if He would show me, *I would do it.* I left Colorado with a vision to either start or work at a camp as my future career.

It was the first time I worked at a camp all summer. I realized what a perfect match it was for my skills and the longings of my heart, having a love for people and for the outdoors. I could see the impact camps had on lives, because I'd listened as campers sat around the campfires talking about the impact of the year before. I wanted to make a difference in peoples' lives, and this seemed like a perfect way.

As soon as I got my first acre and my first dollar, I was ready to get started. As I write about later, that dream became a glorious reality.

That fall I headed back to Bible college in my 1965 Mustang. The four years at Pillsbury were four of the greatest years of my life. I still treasure many of the friendships. The most important thing impressed upon me were the values and principles of God's Word.

I enjoyed being involved in many activities and wasn't one to sit in my room, so I found myself active in almost every facet of college life. I was an officer in our college society, active in the drama department and sports program. I was the monitor of our dorm which meant I was the "cop" who turned in the bad guys. I, being a bit of a trouble maker myself, cut others a lot of slack. I don't think I made any enemies even though I sometimes made the bad guys come to wrestling practice and we would put them in the stretcher hold until they repented!

Following college, I spent three-and-one-half years at Central Seminary in Minneapolis where I received my Masters of Divinity. I felt that since I had committed my life to Christ and to serving Him; the more I knew of the Word of God and how to relate it to people; the more effective I would be. Seminary seemed a natural extension from Bible College for someone with my goals. Later I received my Masters Degree in Guidance/Counseling from Winona State University.

During that time, I had gotten married, worked in heavy construction, traveled four months in Europe, and got involved in youth and camp work whenever possible.

During my four months in Europe I traveled and explored 18 countries. This included visiting six missionaries, going behind the Iron Curtain in Russia, and spending six weeks in Israel. I traveled by train, ship, airplane, motorbike and hitchhiked. Some of the highlights include:

1) Seeing firsthand the tremendous work of overseas missions
2) Touring the countryside and staying with many families I met on the streets or trains
3) Visiting the ancient city of Ephesus in Turkey and doing an archeological dig with some high school students in Jerusalem on Solomon's temple
4) Walking the shores of the sea of Galilee; and
5) Visiting most of the large cities of Europe.

Colorado, College, Seminary and Europe were four tremendous experiences that have helped mold and shape my life. They gave me the tools I needed to make many decisions. I am grateful today for all four of these opportunities.

"Some opportunities that you say 'yes' to become priceless experiences for the rest of your life."

—Bob Bardwell

4

CAULIFLOWER EARS, CRADLES, AND COACHES

"The discipline, work, training, victories, and disappointments in life teach us some of our greatest lessons."

—Bob Bardwell

Sometimes the biggest blessings come through the simplest things. For instance, during my eighth grade year I discovered through tumbling class that I could do flips, round-offs and hand springs with ease. Obviously, I had been gifted with out-standing body control.

Our high school wrestling coach, Howard Sloneker, just happened by one day, and his eye caught me and a few others. He understood the coordination necessary for a good wrestler and a while later he asked me if I would be interested in trying out for the wrestling team. I tipped the scales at 85 pounds soaking wet.

For the next four years I was on the varsity squad, winning far more than losing. I had some disappointing times in wrestling. One I recall was traumatic at the time, but seems humorous as I look back.

I had a bad habit of having my tongue out when it should have been in – like during the third and final period of a wrestling match in my junior year. My head was going down when my opponent's elbow was coming up. With blood running down my face and wrestling tights, I hurried to the local doctor with the end of my tongue held on by only a strand of epidermis. About 40 stitches later, the doctor had my tongue sewn back on. For the next two weeks my tongue was a huge glob of black and blue. I could not talk or chew food. My parents claim it was the quietest it had been in our home since I was born! To this day I still have a dip in my tongue because I had an irritating stitch that was tormenting me, so I pulled it out early. I didn't know the future implications of having a little hole in the middle of my tongue. The worst thing that has happened is the severe burning I experience when a drop of Tabasco sauce lands in it!

Wrestling left another mark on me – literally. One of my wrestling claims to fame is that I have one of those treasured "cauliflower ears" which is caused by not wearing headgear to protect your ears. My ear got smashed into the mat too many times and the tissue in the ear separated and filled in with fluid. The fluid can be drained, but some of it hardens and gives an ear a new, distinctive look.

The fellowship and winning in wrestling were great, but there were struggles which brought deep disappointment. Twice I made it to the state tournament, only to be derailed by something other than superior talent.

During my junior year I had gained a whopping 20 pounds and was wrestling in the 112-pound division. I had won the districts and was in my final match at the regional meet in Owatonna, Minnesota, when, during my match, I blacked out for three minutes. In the meantime I had been pinned! Not only was I disappointed in a loss but also because that meant I was to go to the state tournament as just an alternate. Furthering the disappointment, I was never used.

In my senior year I had won all the dual meets as well as the districts and had good potential of going to state. I won my first three matches in regionals, but during my final match I dislocated my right knee; bringing an end to my high school wrestling career. I was never able to see what my potential might have been at the state level. It seemed I had my share of "almosts" in wrestling which later in life helped to prepare me for other unexpected changes, including my accident seven years later.

_._

> It's easy to let disappointments turn to bitterness and resentment. They will always have an effect on your future. Entertaining such feelings is human nature – harboring them is self-destructive.

_._

I went to Pillsbury Bible College not certain whether my wrestling career would continue. During my freshman year a wrestling program was added and for two years I was the team captain and went undefeated. I still hold the school wrestling record of 75 wins and 4 losses at my alma mater. My winning career was due in part to getting 90% of my take-downs and using the "cradle" as a pinning combination.

I was always cutting weight to balance the scales at weigh-in time the day of the wrestling meets. One of the ways of losing weight was to wear a sweatsuit during practice. Another way was to turn the showers into a sauna. After working up a good sweat, we would open the outside door and roll in the snow in our birthday suits.

My post college wrestling career lasted two more years. I met Olympic twin brothers Jim and Dave Hazewinkel from Anoka, Minnesota. They were the first American wrestlers to both win a medal in the Olympics in Greco Roman wrestling.

I wanted to make the 1972 Olympic team in freestyle wrestling, so I trained with the Hazewinkels at the University of Minnesota while I was attending Central Seminary in Minneapolis. I competed in many tournaments in the midwest to get in shape and sharpen my skills in freestyle.

Jim and Dave, besides being tremendous wrestlers, were bold witnesses for the Lord and shared their love for Christ often. They were respected athletes and always gave the glory to God for their accomplishments. One of Jim's expressions was, "we are tougher than nails," and they lived up to it. To this day, they are still two of my heroes, for their athletic accomplishments and commitments to serve Christ.

The Olympic trials were in Coon Rapids, Minnesota that year, and I was in shape and ready to storm the 142 pound division. I won my first two matches, heightening my hope. I was wrestling an opponent from the University of North Dakota in my third – and last – match before the finals. Suddenly my right knee was again dislocated. Down I went. That was the last match of my career. Another dream had gone astray. Frustrated? Definitely! Now the training, sacrifice and hard work would have to show some rewards in other areas.

It wasn't what I had planned, but I had to move on, accept the situation, and look to the future for other opportunities.

I learned competitiveness, perseverance, and how to win, through wrestling. But I also learned how to lose and how to handle disappointment. The lessons of winning and losing are critical to a person's development, and the lessons from both would be put to valuable use in facing the challenges to come.

5

THE MARATHONS OF L-I-F-E

In the marathons of L-I-F-E, there are no 50-yard lines, no front row seats. Everyone is out on the field. —Bob Bardwell

A marathon is 26.2 grueling, lung-sapping miles averaging approximately 4,000 arm strokes in a wheelchair. Having completed over 70 marathons at the time of this writing, I have some exciting and humorous ventures to share; weaving together the struggles, dreams, disappointments, and challenges into a lesson relating to the marathons we each face in life.

My marathon career started in 1982 when Glen White called and said, "Bob, you've got to come to the 10K Life Run in Rochester and race." I wanted to go because of my competitive and athletic spirit. What Glen didn't know was I didn't want to be associated with the disabled people in wheelchairs. I wanted to go where I was with my able-bodied buddies. This was a big obstacle for me. Up until now, I had never dreamed of hanging out with a group of wheelers who stood out in a crowd.

With a 50-pound Everest and Jennings stainless steel wheelchair, leather farmer gloves, duct tape, water bottle, spare tire, fans, and adrenaline, I showed up at the race. I was filling out the form and noticed they also had a two-mile race. Being naive, I thought when you go to a race, you do every event! I was wrong.

I noticed two strange racing chairs off to the side, but not at the starting line for the two-mile race. The gun went off and four of us stammered off the starting line. Reaching a cruising speed of 12 m.p.h., my front six-inch wheels started to shimmy. I leaned way forward to try and correct the wheels and forgot one of the rules of racing: "Keep your head up and eyes open."

The shimmying came to an abrupt stop in a six-inch pothole and I catapulted forward, landing spread eagle on the blacktop, losing some skin and chewing some gouges in my farmer gloves. The other wheelers just rolled right on by *(no class, man!)* and to my rescue came some runners who tossed me back in the chair and I was off to the races again.

When I crossed the finish line, something inside of me said, "Yes, this is what I want to do." They announced the start of the 10K about ten minutes later. Taping up my blisters, checking my bumps and bruises and gulping down some water, I was at the line for the start of the next race.

Sitting next to me were two "souped up" racing machines. The starting gun went off and the racing chairs were out of sight. One hour and fifteen minutes later, I crossed the finished line. *Overwhelmed* is the best word to describe my emotions. This was the first time since my injury I felt like *I had accomplished something.* I was exhausted! Beside the sore arms, thumping lungs, blisters, and slightly blurred vision, it was the beginning of what I never would have believed: five months later doing my first marathon and setting the goal of completing 100 marathon races.

After that race, I experienced first hand the expression,

"If you don't make dust, you eat dust."

Can you imagine competing in a race, sucking dust down your throat? I vowed, "next race, I'm gonna' make the dust." In reality, that vow was only *nice conversation* without a lot of training and commitment.

Shortly after the race, Glen and I were chatting when he handed me a magazine called *Sports N' Spokes.* I couldn't believe my eyes. I saw a picture of a wheelchair racer crossing the finish line of the Boston Marathon. I read the article about Jim Knaub beating all the runners and before I closed the magazine, I set two goals:

1) Qualify and compete in the Boston Marathon, and,
2) Do a 10K in less than 30 minutes.

I also read an article in *Decision* magazine called "Racing for God," a story of Jim "Magic" Martinson, a double amputee veteran of Vietnam, who also completed the Boston Marathon in his wheelchair. I didn't know how I was going to pull off a marathon after doing a 10K and being completely exhausted, realizing that in a marathon I would have to go 20 more miles!

The following week I called my insurance company and asked if they would like to sponsor me in wheelchair racing. Their first question was, "How much is that going to cost us?" I assured them that my medical costs for them would be less if I trained and kept in good condition. They purchased my first racing chair – a 'Trackmaster' for $1,200.

For the next three years, I pushed approximately 75 miles a week in an effort to reach my goals. Each week I would do one night of hill climbing, one night of sprinting, one night of distance work and one night of interval training. Blisters and sore fingers and hands were a continual problem besides a pressure sore on my rear end (more about that later).

I lost both of my thumbnails from continual pushing and jamming on them. After logging a couple thousand miles in my training journal, I was surprised how much I learned, how much more efficient I became, and how much my speed increased. To this day I still hear racers blaming their chairs for their failures or slow speeds, when in reality, their training effort usually makes the biggest difference.

> When people ask me, "How is your wheelchair racing going?" I usually reply," The chair is just fine, it's the engine that has the problems."

That's not to say the chairs don't require a lot of repair and fine tuning, but it's always easier to blame others, the chair, or our equipment for a disappointing race rather than laziness, not doing homework or putting in enough training.

I reached my goals in my third year of training. My first 10K that I completed in less than thirty minutes was the Kaiser Roll in Minneapolis in July, 1986. I competed in Boston and placed 12th in the wheelchair division out of 75 competitors in 1986 and 10th in 1988.

Parallels between running a marathon and the challenges we face in our daily lives are that:

1. *Each have a beginning and a finish line.*
2. *Neither are a 100-yard dash, but rather a endurance run.*
3. *Both have uphills and downhills, mountains, and valleys.*
4. *Both experience detours, rough roads, and unexpected turns.*
5. *Support is vital to both.*

Four reminders that may help in the marathons you face each day can be remembered by the acronym L.I.F.E.:

34

L – Lift off
I – Inch by inch
F – Fatigue
E – Encouragement

L is for "LIFT OFF"

Getting to the starting line and waiting until the gun goes off is often the hardest part of the task. *'Lift off'* means getting started on the new beginning, making the big decision, starting the new relationship or career, or meeting the unexpected challenge.

I have found three important things to focus on when you are at the starting line: attitude, goals, and equipment.

ATTITUDE

I am devoting a chapter to this subject later, but let me remind you the attitude you choose at the starting line will impact your every step. Chuck Swindoll has wisely written: "Life is 10% what happens to me, and 90% how I react to it."

Remember, you can't start over in life's marathon. You often can't choose your circumstance or situation, but you do have the privilege of choosing your attitude.

GOALS

A goal should be a plan you write down and are willing to work toward. Goals take energy, discipline, blisters, time, and sweat, and often are accompanied with disappointments and delays.

Whether you are shooting for the top ten or are trying to finish before the sun goes down, goals are important. Goals are powerful motivators. Goals give us direction and help us keep our focus. I challenge you to set some worthy goals and to develop an action plan.

---·-·-·-·-·-·-·-·-·-·-·-·-·-·-·-·-

It took
  — **three** years to reach my racing goals,
  — **seven** years to reach the goals I had for
    my Christian camp,
  — **twelve** years to write this book, and
  — **twenty** years to reach my goal of having
    a child.
Each minute of pain, sweat, delay and toil has
been worth it!

---·-·-·-·-·-·-·-·-·-·-·-·-·-·-·-·-

EQUIPMENT

As important as what you take along or wear in a race is what you don't take. Hebrews 12:1 reads, "Throw off everything that hinders…and run with perseverance." In a wheelchair race, what you show up with at the starting line will strongly impact the outcome of the race. Such things as the condition of your racing chair, properly taped gloves, water bottles, spare tires, etc.

Baggage we need to "throw off" includes: negative attitudes, a lifestyle of questionable choices which lead to later regrets, and the "hurry syndrome" in which we are too busy to adore the daisies currently in front of us because there *may be* a rose garden one hundred yards ahead.

Some of the proper equipment that comes into play in life's marathons include your family, support groups, education, friends, values, spiritual life, and experience.

Check out your equipment. It's important!

I is for "INCH BY INCH"

Inch-by-inch, step-by-step, block-by-block, mile-by-mile is the way you finish a marathon. Minute-by-minute, hour-by-hour, day-by-day, year-by-year is the way we live our lives.

When you break a marathon down mile-by-mile, it keeps the 26-plus miles ahead of you in perspective.

> Success in finishing your marathon is determined by two principles: pacing yourself and keeping your focus.

When I start a marathon, it would be foolish to sprint for as long as I can. I am told that a race car driver named Mickey Thompson started the Indianapolis 500 more than 10 times. He always went out fast, but never finished the race.

Pacing yourself means you have a long way to go, so hold back, keep some strength in reserve, listen to your body, and keep that steady, persistent push.

Keeping your focus is vital, or you will waste energy on secondary matters. Losing your focus in a race will always keep you from doing your best. In a marathon, there are plenty of interruptions, distractions, and unexpected things to get us off our focus.

I'll never forget in one of the Twin Cities Marathon races, Jim Martinson and George Murray traded the lead for 26 miles of the race. The final 385 yards were mostly downhill. Murray was in front in the sprint to the finish line, but he allowed himself to be distracted by looking over his shoulder to see if Martinson was in the draft. As he looked over his left shoulder, Martinson was passing him on the right. By the time Murray turned back and saw Martinson, it was too late and Martinson won in a photo finish.

> How is your focus? Have you been distracted?
> Let down your guard? Have you forgotten to
> take one step at a time? Are you off the course?
> Are you looking over your left shoulder?

I heard the story of a college student who graduated with high honors. When he was a child he felt strongly that he wanted to become a medical missionary. Following his graduation, he received several high paying offers from big businesses. After turning down each offer, one company president called him and offered to raise his salary even higher. His response was, "Your salary is high enough, but your mission isn't what I'm called to do."

That young man was focused, and he allowed nothing – even material wealth – to distract him. *Philippians 3:14: "I press on toward the goal to win the prize."*

Prior to his crucifixion, Jesus kept His focus on what He was called to do when He said in Luke 22:42, "Father, if you are willing, take this cup from me, yet not my will, but yours be done."

F is for "FATIGUE"

We all get tired and want to throw in the towel. I'm often rudely introduced to 'fatigue' earlier than I want in a marathon. When we get tired, we're tempted to quit and/or compromise.

The first temptation may be to quit when we get tired. It's human nature. Winston Churchill said, "Never, never, never give up." When we get tired, those high goals, moral commitments and standards, and promises, all get challenged.

When I want to quit, I remind myself of the words of Paul in Galatians 6:9: "Don't become weary of doing right, for in due season, you will reap if you do not quit."

You may overcome the temptation to quit but be tempted to give in to *compromise*. Don't do it! When I get tired in a race, and drop back from the pace, I'm forced to compromise my top-ten chances and take what place I can get. Murphy's law must happen to every marathoner:

1) things take longer than I thought;
2) things aren't as easy as I thought and;
3) when things can go wrong, they will.

In life, when we are physically or emotionally tired, we must be on guard against compromising what is important to us. The standards and values we have been taught take courage to uphold. Take heart. In a marathon, there is hopefully a rest stop around the corner. In life, you may need a day off. Maybe the next day you will be surprised with a downhill!

E is for "ENCOURAGEMENT"

I have heard it said, "The common cold of human emotions is discouragement." A race is hardly a race, or at best has few strong finishers, without encouragers along the way. You can encourage people with words, letters, phone calls, hugs, listening, and example. When you speak, are your words true, kind and up-lifting?

I have heard it said, "It's not how far you fall, but how high you bounce."

There are few better ways to bring a big bounce into someone's life than to be an encourager. Think of the people in your life who are facing a difficult challenge. Many may be broken, unmotivated, jobless, or struggling with marriages and relationships. They need your encouragement. Remember, well done is better than well said.

In nature, geese are one of our greatest role models when it comes to encouragement.

A Lesson from the Geese
Taken from "Christ's Communique"
As each bird flaps its wings, it creates an "uplift"
for the bird following. By flying in a V formation, the

whole flock adds 71% more flying range than if each bird flew alone.

People who share a common direction and sense of community can get where they are going quicker and easier when they are traveling on the thrust of one another.

Whenever a goose falls out of formation, it suddenly feels the drag and resistance of trying to fly alone, and quickly gets back in formation to take advantage of the "lifting power" of the bird immediately in front.

If we have as much sense as a goose, we will stay in formation with those who are headed where we want to go.

When the lead goose gets tired, it rotates back into the formation and another goose flies at the point position.

It pays to take turns doing the hard work and sharing leadership – interdependent with each other.

The geese in formation honk from behind to encourage those up front to keep their speed.

We need to make sure our honking from behind is encouraging, not something less helpful.

When a goose gets sick or wounded or shot down, two geese drop out of formation and follow him down to help protect him. They stay with him until he is either able to fly again or dies, then they launch out on their own with another formation or to catch up with the flock.

If we have as much sense as the geese, we'll stand by each other like that.

Never let a day go by without encouraging someone. I shared my story at a church in Faribault, Minnesota. Three years later I got a call from someone who attended that meeting. He said, "Bob, you don't know me, but my name is Gary Hoganson. You spoke at our church three years ago and inspired me to run a marathon someday. Well, this is the year. I have been training and plan to run the Twin Cities Marathon. I also plan to get pledges and make it a fund-raiser for your camp." Wow! He raised $500 for the camp. You never know what a word of encouragement can do.

6

WINNING ISN'T ALWAYS FIRST PLACE

When you get what you want in your struggle for self
And the world makes you king for a day
Just go to the mirror and look at yourself
And see what that person has to say.

For it isn't your father, mother, brother or sister
whose judgment upon you must pass
The person whose verdict counts most in our life
Is the one staring back from the glass.
—Author Unknown

I had just finished my first athletic competition in twelve years, and I thought my mission for the day was complete. Second place. Wow! What a good feeling. I thought I had learned a lot about myself, about rekindling the competitive flame, about being a good finisher.

But I would learn much more that day. I would enhance my definition of winning.

I had competed in a novice 5K race that day. Afterwards, I quickly refreshed myself and took a spot inches from the starting line for the 10K race. I wanted to see the veteran racers and hopefully learn something from their performance.

I remember looking back in the racing pack and seeing people with disabilities far worse than myself lined up to race. I couldn't help wondering why they even came to the race. They didn't have a chance of winning first place. What were they here for?

As the gun went off, the more experienced and elite racers quickly took the lead. I felt consumed by helplessness as I watched the more physically challenged racers struggle in their wake. Some had only one arm with which to push and steer. Quadriplegics that didn't even have hands or fingers to grip the rims had to rely on the back of their wrists to turn the wheels. I wanted to reach out and help them.

I felt strangely fortunate for having the use of my entire upper body. For some people, it took more courage and strength to get to the starting line than it did for me to get to the finish line.

I waited approximately 30 minutes at the finish line and watched the faces of those who came in first, second and third. I shared their rush of adrenaline. As I watched those that followed, I saw no discernible difference in the grin on their face or the light in their eyes. As the last wheeler pushed across the finish line in her modified everyday chair, I watched her face light up with as much exhilaration as the one who came in first

43

place. For her, winning wasn't only first place.

Watching her finish enhanced my definition of winning. Besides first place winners, there are second-, third-, and fourth-place winners, as well. The winners that day were those who 1) did their best 2) didn't quit and 3) delighted in finishing.

As I watched the faces of the racers cross the finish line, I learned a valuable lesson that one can be a *winner* everyday of their life. It's great when you can capture that first place crown, and that is always to be our goal, but there are other types of victories, many often more for character-building than for a first place finish.

That was the day I learned that those who cross the finish line *first* aren't the only ones who should be called winners. This chapter is written for those who don't always come in first place, but who get involved and finish.

My winning wrestling career both in high school and college allowed me to experience the celebrated emotion of a hand raised in victory. After my accident, I thought my athletic career, with all its thrill and excitements of victory, had abruptly ended. With Glen White's introduction to wheelchair racing, the competative fires were rekindled, evoking treasured memories of the moments as winner on the wrestling mat.

KAISER ROLL

That wheelchair race that redefined "winners" was the Kaiser Roll 5K and 10K, held annually in Bloomington. This race is dubbed one of the largest 10K international wheelchair races. I had never seen an authentic wheelchair racing event and being a novice, signed up for the 5K.

The night before the race I struggled to find sleep in a myriad of insecurities. Often I woke to check the clock. The time would soon be here to 'roll out' into the competitive arena — only this time I wasn't entering as a seasoned champion. There were no past laurels on which to rest. The risk of losing that portion of my identity was a real possibility. Was I ready to accept the challenge, to test my abilities against other athletes, perhaps better athletes than myself? What if my performance fell short of my wrestling triumphs?

I struggled with the thought of losing my past identity as being a first place winner. With my head on the pillow, staring at the ceiling, thoughts of doubt crept in… *maybe I don't have the ability in this sport.*

It was 5 a.m. when Russ Halverson (a 14-year-old training buddy, who came along as part of my 'pit crew') and I left for the 100-mile drive to Bloomington. During the drive, I tried to visualize every mile of the race; anticipating every phase of the quest and trying to imagine what it would be like. When we pulled into the restaurant parking lot where the race would begin, I couldn't believe my eyes. Nothing in my wildest imagination could have prepared me for what I saw and felt.

Hundreds of people in wheelchairs swarmed the parking lot, many with similar disabilities to mine, but some with far different. As I steered my car through the mass, I felt myself emerge into another world, a familiar world, a world where people with disabilities was the norm and not the exception.

I suddenly realized I was whole, and whether I was physically whole or not didn't matter. What mattered was that I was alive and soon to roll up to the starting line.

As I got out of my car I felt the energy surround me. The air was filled with the excited drones of voices as athletes and crew members prepared for the races.

I willingly blended with the scurry of movement. The fever of competition was on everyone's brow. I rolled my "Trackmaster" racing machine to the registration tables, eager to pick up my packet with my racing number. I was already making mental notes to inflate my tires, check my Velcro straps, and secure my water bottle, which had a quarter-inch water line coming from the bottle to my mouth. Valuable time would be lost if I used my hands for anything other than pushing.

The 'saddling' ceremony had begun. I fastened my number to my sky-blue lycra racing jersey and put several rounds of tape on my gloves to keep the blisters to a minimum.

The road, lined by people and bobbing balloons overhead, was cleared by police officers. A hush fell over the crowd.

After the starting gun went off I quickly reached a cruising speed of 14 m.p.h. I knew very little about drafting behind others or working together to gain more speed. I just kept doing the only thing I knew how to do, pushing on those 13-inch pushrims until my muscles and lungs felt like they were going to explode. I wanted to be part of the pack. I wanted to be counted. I wanted to be a first place winner.

With less than a half-mile to the finish line, I jockeyed back and forth for position with several other wheelers. However, one wheeler had pulled way out in front and was out of reach. I was determined to capture second place. With steady and intense pushing, I crossed the finish line in second place with a time of 17 minutes and 50 seconds. Winded and tired, I was filled with an indescribable feeling of accomplishment.

It wasn't just a race I had completed. It was a celebration for all the training and preparation that had gone into making this moment happen.

As I finished my first race, I realized that I had only just begun in the sport I so quickly came to love.

DO YOUR BEST

Those who achieve first place deserve respect and first place honors. Their accomplishments set standards for which the rest of us must strive toward. But the lesson to everyone is to understand the significance of striving to **do your best**.

It is often in striving that we discover life's purpose. Some of life's greatest lessons we learn come from being ready, willing, and prepared to

> accept whatever challenge is put before us each
> day. It's a commitment of doing our best.

I believe everyone can be a winner.

We are all in the same race. It is called, *The Marathon of Life*. There are no 50-yard line seats in this marathon.

God expects every ounce of effort from us, but also promises, *"...and your strength will equal your days"* Deuteronomy 33:25. The emphasis is not on the prize, but the attitude with which we run. The emphasis should be on doing our best, but always with first place as the goal. Trust that He will guide you toward the special purpose He has and that He will never put anything before you which you cannot handle.

In Colossians 3:23 we are reminded, *"Whatever you do, work at it with all your heart."* When you cross the finish line of life, God is more interested in the spirit and attitude of how you ran, and if you did your best, than in counting the number of first place trophies you have collected. Out of nearly 250 races I achieved more than 90 first place finishes. When I came home from a race my friends would usually ask, "Bob, did you win?" Of course what they really meant was, "Did you get first place?" Winning is primarily only associated with first place in our culture.

> I always told them I won — and then I let them
> know what place I finished.

For three consecutive years I held the first place title for winning the Twin Cities Marathon (1986-88) and I will cherish that memory forever. However, other memories are just as special.

On of them is the completion of my first marathon, the Twin Cities Marathon in 1983. I finished fourth and was overwhelmed with joy, overshadowing my sore and tired muscles. In preparation for that race, I competed in a half-marathon (13.1 miles). It was a race called the "Mad Dash to Moscow" held in Austin, Minnesota. Moscow is a small town outside of Austin which boasts a population of 14+. (The plus sign is because, during the census, a local farmer's goats were due to deliver and a plus sign was added in anticipation of additional 'kids'.)

Approximately 100 runners and four wheelers showed up to compete. Tony Possehl, my training partner, took the lead with my brother-in-law, Joel Raygor, who was riding a bicycle as our support crew and encourager. During the entire race I was *"eating dust"* as I struggled to keep up with Tony, who finished a couple blocks ahead of me. I had a hard time convincing myself I was only half-tired in preparation for the 26.2 mile marathon.

> I reminded myself: "I can't always be the best, but I can always do my best." When you do your best, no matter what the outcome, there is satisfaction in knowing that you fully extended yourself.

The other memorable race was at Grandma's Marathon in 1984 in which I crossed the finish line after having three flat tires during the race, lessons of which I will share later. Neither the Twin Cities Marathon nor Grandma's Marathon were first place finishes for me, but they were satisfying because I could say, "I did my best."

Do Your Best

Just do your best in whatever you do
though sometimes it may not be easy for you.
Just do your best, that's all one can ask,
in spite of the odds, whatever the task.
Just do your best with what you have got,
And if it's a little or if it's a lot,
You'll know in your heart when each day is through,
You've done everything God expected of you.
> —Grace E. Easily

DON'T QUIT

Besides doing your best, winning is also not quitting. Sometimes the victory is maintaining the fight. You may even have had good reason to quit, but as the sticker on the front of my wheelchair says, *"Run the race and never give up."*

Learning not to quit during difficult pursuits seems to be a lifelong lesson for me. As far back as high school, I can recall my wrestling coach having to give me a few strong words of encouragement during the third period of a match, when my brain was sending cardiac arrest messages to my heart. "Keep your head up," the coach would yell. "Coach, I'm not keeping it down on purpose, my opponent happens to be cramming my face in the mat." The coach knows that when your shoulder is on the mat, you have become vulnerable to quitting.

I learned a lesson about not quitting after my first test in college. I drove home and announced to my parents that I wasn't college material, and that I planned to drop out.

> They reminded me, "Son, you never quit just because you've failed something. Make it your challenge, things can only get better."

I headed back to college Monday morning in my 1965 Mustang, and things did get better. I was oblivious to the significance of what a decision to quit college might have meant to my future. Today, I'm grateful to my high school coach, my parents, and the counsel of God's Word that exhorted me to "keep my head up" in times of disappointment and trial.

You can never be sure when, what seems like a small act or decision at the time, may profoundly affect your future and someone else's life.

The Grandma's Marathon memory which I referred to earlier is a good lesson in perseverance. Before the race, I was warming up by pushing my racing chair up and down the highway, when suddenly I heard a pop. Oh, no, flat tire. It was about ten minutes until the start of the race and I had to fix a flat tire and get past 6,000 anxious runners as they stood between me and the start line. I had come prepared with an extra tube and air pump, but the timing was bad. Tony, my racing competitor, and Larry, a friend who had driven us to the race, quickly came to the rescue with the tube, a pump and screwdriver. We scrambled to get the new tube in, hoping for a routine fix. Larry began pumping, but the tire didn't inflate. "Pump harder," I yelled anxiously. The harder he pumped, the more the air came out in every direction. We had pinched the tube with the screwdriver, and so I sat with a flat tire.

> Tony rolled off to the starting line, and I sat discouraged by the side of the road. I heard the starting gun go off, and now I knew that the months of training and the effort to make the trip were wiped out.

At that moment I looked up and saw a boy about 11 years old riding toward me on a bicycle. I stared at his tire. "Hey buddy," I shouted, "I came to race today, but have had two flat tires. Would you happen to have a tube that I could use?" The boy jumped off his bike and unzipped the fanny pack he had strapped to the back of his seat.

"You can have it," he said. He pulled out a tube as I watched in disbelief.

"Does it have any holes in it?" I asked.

"Not that I can remember," he said with a grin. I thanked him and took the tube. We had to do a bit of coercing to get the tube inside the tire, but finally our efforts paid off. Celebration time! Air in the tires, body in the chair, gloves on, and I was on the road again.

I passed as many runners as I could and was trying to catch up to the slower wheelers. I was nearing mile six when I felt a slight bump on the left wheel. I put my hand down on the tire and felt the bump with every revolution. I looked down, and to my dismay, the tube was bulging out near the valve and was ready to explode.

Quickly, I pulled to the side of the road and let out some air before the tube popped. There I sat with my third flat tire. Runners zipped past and offered words of encouragement. I

shouted to some elderly spectators who were sitting on lawn chairs across the road. I told them of my misfortune and asked if, by chance, they had an air pump.

"No, but I'll go up to the house and check," one of them said. I maneuvered my way across the road, avoiding runners, and by the time I reached the other side, there was the man with an old black tire pump. I got out of my chair to realign the tire, took the pump, and soon, to my amazement, I had a tire full of air again. I thanked them for being good Samaritans and was back on the road in less than five minutes. *Snip dingle.* Twenty miles later I rolled across the finish line with a story to tell to my grandkids.

Driving home later that day, I was reminded of the story in the New Testament when the disciples had only two fish and a little bread offered by a young boy to feed 5,000 hungry people. This was an impossible feat for the disciples to accomplish and their solution was to send the crowd home in the face of what seemed impossible. Jesus took the fish and bread and blessed it and everyone had a meal with leftovers.

> Yes, sometimes when things seem impossible and you're ready to quit, a boy on a bicycle shows up with a spare tube in his fanny pack.

At times you can be tempted to quit because the circumstances of a situation aren't what you expected. That was the case in my third marathon, the Whitewater Marathon in St. Charles, Minnesota, in 1985. I didn't find out until three days before the race that 13 miles of the race were on a gravel road. To add a little intensity to the test, the temperatures soared to a sweltering 90 degrees plus for the day. In Minnesota (noted for its insufferable humidity), that's a prescription for heatstroke in the shade.

There were six wheelchair racing entries, including myself, who gathered to discuss the option of pulling out of the race at mile 13 where the gravel begins. Finally, one wheeler said, "I came this far, I'm doing the 26.2 miles." His eyes darted back and forth but no one wanted to be the one to "*wimp out.*" With that challenge, we all donned a couple more sweatbands, topped off the water bottles and lined up for the race.

The gravel was there to greet us at mile 13. The wheels on my Trackmaster rocked laboriously over the gravel with each stroke. The inconsistency of the gravel caused the chair to list violently, and I had to concentrate just to maintain my balance at times. Sweat from my palms permeated my gloves. I felt the sun scorching through my jersey. I tried to ignore the imposing obstacles and focus on the words 'stick to it.' It was like hearing coach's voice again: "Keep your head up." At last, I passed the 26 mile mark and the last two tenths of a mile were downhill. The word "downhill" is usually sweet music to a wheeler, but not on gravel! Four of us crossed the finish line and will always be blessed with the knowledge that when things got tough on that hot summer day, *we didn't quit.*

DELIGHT IN FINISHING

It is not the blistering pace in which you begin a race that's important. It's whether you keep your focus and pace yourself to the finish line. That's true with anything you do in life. What would the world be like if people never completed the things they began?

Louis Pasteur almost perfects pasteurization.

The colonies almost secede from England.

Jesus Christ almost gives His life on the cross for our sins.

There is joy in finishing. The word itself brings a sigh of relief and accomplishment. Coming around the last turn in a marathon, hearing those shouts and cheers from the finish line, seems to draw me like the outgoing tide in a thrust of newfound energy. It's the home stretch.

> I look up and see that big finish line banner flapping in the breeze, and then I cross that thin piece of masking tape on the road that figuratively says, "You did it; you finished."

The months of training, discouragements, and sacrifice are behind me for a moment while I enjoy the sweet victory of calling myself a finisher.

In the New Testament, the Apostle Paul was a finisher. He said in II Timothy 4:7, *"I have fought the good fight, I have finished the race"*.

The important thing is to be heading in the right direction on the right road and to never give up. The experience of a friend of mine best illustrates the point.

Bob Wieland, who had both of his legs amputated, finished the New York City Marathon. While Bob was scooting along on his arms down the streets, he was stopped by a police officer and asked what he thought he was doing out in this dangerous traffic.

"I'm competing in the New York marathon," Bob replied.

"Well, sir," said the officer in a abrupt voice, "The NYC marathon ended three days ago, and you're dead last. Now, you better get off the road."

"No" Bob argued. "I'm not last. I'm in front of four million New Yorkers who never showed up at the starting line."

Bob finished!

Jesus Christ didn't give up when they shouted, *"Crucify Him"* Matthew 27:23. Jesus had the power to call 10,000 angels and set him free, but He didn't. He completed what He had come to do – die and take the judgement for our sins. Jesus Christ's last words were, *"It is finished."* How about you? Do you have unfinished business you have been avoiding? Could there be something you have started and have chosen to quit?

Maybe you have "dropped out" or "thrown in the towel" and felt up to this point that finishing wasn't an option.

Make a commitment today to pick up where you left off and complete what God has put before you. Yes, you can make a fresh start. If you're off course, come back. God wants you to be a finisher and will empower you to reach the finish line.

7

HEARTBREAK HILL HITTING THE WALL

Don't Quit
When things go wrong as they sometimes will,
and the road you're traveling seems all uphill.
When your funds are low, and your debts are high
and you want to smile, but you have to sigh.
When care is pressing you down a bit,
rest if you must, but never QUIT.

Author Unknown

If you haven't experienced a 'heartbreak hill' in your life, get ready, because it's just around the corner.

"HEARTBREAK HILL" - This is the name of the famous hill close to mile 21 in the Boston Marathon. I know, I have climbed it (I mean, crept up it) five times and can assure you the name is very appropriate.

"HITTING THE WALL" - This is the all-too-well-known expression at mile 20 in a marathon, where your body tells you it's quitting time. It not only feels it, but tells you in no uncertain terms, "It's time to 'hang it up' or 'lay it down' — as in the medical tent.

For me, climbing HEARTBREAK HILL, went something like this:

With my head down, not wanting to see how steep the hill is, I'm pushing one stroke at a time. Watching my digital computer in the m.p.h mode, it reads anywhere from 0 to 5 (battery must be dead!). I can't believe it, those cracks and specks in the blacktop seem to be going by so slow! Shoulders burning, wrists and forearms stinging, heart banging away, and vision a bit blurry, it's time to call for help. The runners seem to have a bit more power on the uphills, and they move one step at a time right on past me. Finally, after I'm exhausted, I figure it's worth a try, so as a runner is cruising past, I yell, 'Hey buddy, you're doing a good job, how about a push?' Now, it's illegal, but just maybe he might feel sorry for this poor tired disabled person, and give me a push. Wrong! It never happens. He's tired, too, and does something better than a push, yelling back, "You can do it!" So, it's back to one more stroke. After a couple of hundred strokes, I look up to find I've reached the top of the hill. If I'm lucky, on the other side is what I call a "Make room for Bob to zoom" situation. Here's where the cruising takes place.

With elbows in and head tucked, I watch the m.p.h. figure increase! 10... 15... 20... 25... 30-plus. (Battery is fine!) The tired runners are yelling, "Look out for the wheelers!" About half way down, I meet up with that runner who turned me down for a push. "Hey, buddy, how about a ride," he says. "Sorry, remember that hill back there, see you later." We are not really competing against the runners, because we have our own division. When I get a chance, its always fun to chat and do a few hundred yards with them.

Only on one hill did ever I quit pushing and come to a stop. I was racing in Faribault, Minnesota and part of the course went through a golf course. There was a short, but very steep hill. I stopped, started to roll backwards, panicked, and locked up the brakes. Over backwards I went! Thankfully, a golfer lifted me back up, gave me a push, and I was back on the trail again.

Most every marathon at mile 20 has a large wall built with an arch to run through. Sometimes a big arch of balloons is over the wall, and there are lots of people holding signs letting the athletes know they can make it. It's a very encouraging point in the race, and passing through rejuvenates you to make the last six-plus miles.

So what about life's marathons with its heartbreak hills and walls to hit? Everyone reading these words is out on the course, and some of you will be right in the midst of your heartbreak - with a strong headwind. Maybe you are soon to face it and are sure you are going to hit the wall.

Others of you at the moment are on the downhill side, zooming along in life and all seems to be going well. GREAT. That's the way we all like it. However, remember to be grateful to God and others who have encouraged you and will be there for you when you face the next uphill.

HEARTBREAK FOR TONY!

In 1988, as Tony Possehl and I were approaching Heartbreak Hill at mile 20 at the Boston Marathon, Tony suddenly grabbed his chest. What a frightening experience! He only had enough energy to go half speed. I wheeled with him as we started up the hill. He told me to go on because he would be a bit slower. About 25 minutes after I crossed the finish, here came Tony. He looked miserable, felt miserable, and said he needed to go to the hotel and lay down. The chest pain never let up, so we took Tony to the airport and he flew back home. Checking in at a local hospital, they quickly called Mayo One, a helicopter from the Mayo Clinic in Rochester, and rushed him to the emergency room. He had had an aneurism of the heart. The aorta had ballooned and he actually had a heart attack on Heartbreak Hill. Today Tony is doing fine with a few replacement parts and is my constant competitor.

My friend, hopefully your heart hasn't given out due to the struggles and steep hills you are facing. Two great resources have gotten me up steep hills and have kept me going when I hit life's wall:

1) God - I have chosen to look to him at these times and rely on promises like Isaiah 40:30-31: "Even youths grow tired and weary, and young men stumble and fall; but those who hope in the Lord will renew their strength." I also lean on Matthew 11:28: "Come to me, all you who are weary and burdened, and I will give you rest."

2) Other People - Along the Boston Marathon course are thousands of fans, spectators, and friends all cheering you along to the finish line. At Heartbreak Hill especially, they crowd together so densely the street is often narrowed. Why? They know that this is where you need the most encouragement. They know this is where you will weaken and thoughts of quitting rumble through the mind. So they are there for support, holding up signs, playing in bands, exhausting themselves as they yell 'Keep it up!'

Many encouragers have been there for me, and I trust you are surrounded by people who love you no matter what your situation or what you have done. You don't have to endorse what someone has done if it is wrong, but you can support and love the *person*. This seems to be what God is telling me in Galatians 6:2, *"Carry each other's burdens,"* and in Romans 12:15, *"Rejoice with those who rejoice; mourn with those who mourn."*

8

CHEERLEADERS, CHARACTERS AND CRASHES

Life at its best is fragile and short!
—Copied

Wheelchairs are not allowed on the escalators!

When the starting gun goes off in a marathon, one of the few stops made are at the water stations. Though they are often called water stations, let me tell you a few more appropriate names for them: 1) Oasis, that middle of the desert pit stop, 2) Water cup capitol of the world. Thousands of cups of water and other refreshing drinks are being suspended at the end of the fingertips of the volunteers ready for consumption.

When the wheelers come through the water stops, the scene takes on a dramatic change.

With their toes behind the line, body leaning forward at 90 degrees and arms outstretched, it's unclear whether volunteers are trying to keep their toes from getting run over or from getting soaked when the cup of water hits the hand of the wheeler and soaks down his face, jersey, and pushrims. If lucky, one can even get a swallow out of the ordeal!

I can tell the volunteers who have encountered wheelers before – they start running alongside and hand over a full cup of water. Oh, does that quench the thirst! But, if you have had a few thousand runners pass one of these water stations before you get there, beware! Cups are everywhere. Piles of cups, some still with water, start scattering as wheelers bulldoze through them. Before I get to a water station, I usually drink from my water bottle so I don't have the craving for water.

From leaning forward most of the race with my chin nearly resting on my knees, my back gets a bit fatigued. (Actually, my lower back is occasionally killing me!) I don't know if I have been bending the Harrington Rods along my spine, but at times my lower back pain registers at about a seven on the spinal cord Richter scale. Instead of getting water, I always ask jokingly, "Are any chiropractors available?" The answer is always the same, "Sorry, check at the finish line." So, I sit up straight, take a few deep breaths and hit the trail.

_ . _ . _ . _ . _ . _ . _ . _ . _ . _ . _ . _ . _ . _

"Where there is a wheel, there is a way."

_ . _ . _ . _ . _ . _ . _ . _ . _ . _ . _ . _ . _ . _

Along the way there are clowns and cheerleaders risking laryngitis to help you reach your goal. They're great! Just about the time my energy is on empty, out from nowhere a band will start up, or someone will yell, "You can do it" or "You're looking good." I always yell back, "You are too."

I had some fans at one race holding up Ironwood Springs Christian Ranch T-shirts as they were cheering me on. What an encouragement.

BLANCHE'S STORY

One of the most determined and fiery competitors I've ever met is a young man named Craig Blanchette while at the first Wheels of Fire wheelchair race in 1986 at Seattle, Washington. From Eugene, Oregon, Blanche was born with legs only to just above the knee. Sitting near me in Husky Stadium waiting for the awards, Blanche had with him a "Shadow" racing wheelchair. I found out later he was friends with Jim Martinson, the builder of these chairs and owner of the company "Magic in Motion." Jim introduced me to Blanche and we chatted a bit. He had a girl sitting on his lap however, so our conversation was rather brief.

Blanche, as he liked to be called, had finally found a sport at which he could excel and was anticipating a great race. With a knack for finding psychological advantages, he had a special T-shirt printed just for the race. On the back across the shoulders, it said in large, bold letters: **"SURPRISE."**

When he caught the lead pack, he stayed with them for a time, just long enough for them to get the message. He dropped back a bit, but finished very strong. He heard that the next big race was in Phoenix and he boasted he would take home the prize money from the race. Of course, showing up at the starting line without an appropriate T-shirt would be uncool. So Blanche had another T-shirt printed saying in big bold letters across the shoulders: **"REMEMBER ME?"** Well, they did remember Blanche, at least after the race when he pulled away at a sprint to the finish and rolled across claiming the prize money.

Blanche and I became friends and would see each other again soon. The next race on the circuit was the Gasparilla in Tampa, Florida. This was George Murray country. George, from Tampa, had won this race about six years in a row and was the founder and owner of a racing wheelchair company called "Top End."

George had wheeled his chair across the USA and was the

WE'RE HAPPY
YOU WON THE
CHICAGO
MARATHON!

THANKS FOR
THE GOOD TIME
AT IRONWOOD!

Hi, Bart—

Saw the clip on Channel 11 the other night — You deserve all the credit you receive!

You do more than let miracles happen, you are one yourself & create even more.

I think of you often — God bless you!

Bob – age 6

Parents – Lester and Jeanne Bardwell

College wrestling team (I'm third from the left)

College work day

My trail horse named Pepsi
at Horn Creek Ranch

Northern Minnesota
bear hunt

"HOW DO YOU DIVIDE YOUR
   LOVE AMONG FOUR CHILDREN?"
"I DON'T DIVIDE IT—
      I MULTIPLY IT!"

first wheeler to be pictured on the front of "Wheaties" cereal boxes. To knock off George would be quite a feat. But Blanche arrived in Tampa very determined. I saw him at the hotel and he said, "Hey Bart, I gotta' show you my special T-shirt for the race." It read: **"HURRY MURRAY."**

The gun went off and Blanche stayed with the front pack, which included George. The final sprint after the last turn included Blanche, George, and Andre' Viger of Canada. Andre' and George, being old racing buddies with all the experience and strategy, felt they had the margin. Wrong. Blanche sensed the blocking tactics and powered around them, cruising past George and Andre' with his hands held in victory, as George read the message Blanche had specially prepared for him: "Hurry Murray."

ANOTHER KIND OF HEARTBREAK HILL!

Once, after the Wheels of Fire in Seattle, several of us decided to go up to Crystal Mountain and coast back down a six mile stretch of the road. We were reaching speeds up to 30 m.p.h. in our regular wheelchairs. When we got to the bottom of the mountain, Blanche, along with Jim "Magic" Martinson and Tim Clark, decided to hang on to the bumper of the van, and go back up Crystal Mountain. I was sitting in the back of the van with the rear trunk gate open telling them when we reached 30 m.p.h. Three wheelchairs tightly together going this fast behind a van just isn't advisable. Suddenly, their rear wheels touched and in a split second they all crashed. Magic and Blanche, being double amputees, just tucked and rolled and came out with only scratches. Tim, a paraplegic, was trashed, being all scraped up, laying on the road, and whining in pain. I'm sure he was singing, "Oh, to be an amputee." At first, we thought he was dead.

We scraped them all off the road, got them loaded into the van, and called it another venture.

Today, Blanche is one of the regulars at our National

Wheelchair Sports and Recreation Camp held each July. Blanche and his wife Anita are the parents of two boys, Quincy and Lexi. He has gone on to be one of the dominate wheelchair athletes in the world.

A WHEELERS LAMENT

Pushing and rolling to get into shape
Biceps straining just testing fate.
Out on the road so early in the morning,
Cars swerving at you without any warning.

With taped up gloves and a full water bottle,
Through wind and rain, I give it full throttle.
Catching other wheelers, oh, what a thrill,
Lord, give me strength for just one more hill.

Meantime, a hungry dog who's not had lunch,
Elbow hamburger he'll try to munch.
The body is strong, my mind is clear,
Bring on the day, I have no fear.

— Bob Bardwell

DIAMOND HEAD DISASTER

The agility of wheelers is vastly limited compared to runners, so when we encounter a problem on the course, it's not always easy to stay in the chair! I've taken my share of tumbles. Once, in Honolulu, I was drafting behind my broad-shouldered friend Mike King. When Mike and I went downhill (I was in the tuck position behind Mike, bumping him forward), we would fly past the solo chairs like they were rolling backwards.

At mile 18 we had just completed a loop (Hawaii Kai) and were going to make a sharp right turn coming off a downhill and go back on the same road we came out on. As we came around the dangerous and fast curve, there were two slower racers coming toward us head on.

In such traffic split-second decisions are required. One of the wheelers swerved in front of me to avoid another collision. We hit head on, did 360s in the air, and landed hard on the concrete.

The 'Search and Destroy' team - I mean, rescue squad - came with a van and scraped us off the road. I was not hurt badly - just minor scrapes and cuts - so I sat at the finish line waiting for Mike to cross. I chatted with Sally, the race director, and asked her if I could get the finisher awards. I told her, "It says in the rules that you have to finish the race, but it doesn't say you have to finish it in a wheelchair." She laughed and said, "I guess you're right." I had gone 18 miles in the wheelchair and another eight in the van.

I kept waiting for Mike, but didn't see him. I knew something had happened. In another 10 minutes, Mike finally came in, bruised and scraped up. His jersey was all ripped up, his shoulder, arm, hip and side of his leg were 'road rash.'

Mike explained: "I was coming down Diamond Head Mountain at about 40 m.p.h. when I blew a rear tire. I lost control of the chair and bounced from side to side of the street until I finally stopped." As I listened to Mike's story, I was glad my crash happened at mile 18. Do you know where I would have been, coming down Diamond Head Mountain if I hadn't crashed earlier? About six inches behind Mike, and we would have been going faster. Both Mike and I learned some important lessons and were a bit more careful since that race.

WAIKIKI WEDDING

My next experience in Honolulu was much more pleasant. Just a few hours after the marathon, I had the privilege of performing a wedding ceremony down at Wakiki beach for a wheelchair racing friend, Rapheal Ibarra and his finance, Kay. Rapheal had just gotten runner-up in the marathon a few hours earlier. It was a beautiful ceremony on the beach. Rapheal, who was from the Los Angeles area, had attended our wheelchair sports camp in the summer and our friendship with him and Kay had grown over the years. Today they are living in Alabama and Rapheal is working for a wheelchair company.

Meanwhile, I'm waiting for my next Waikiki Wedding invitation.

THE BIG ONE . . .

The biggest crash came in 1987 at the Boston Marathon. At the time there were no rules for wearing helmets, perhaps because there had been no serious injuries. As approximately 75 elite wheelers sat anxiously at the starting line waiting for the starting gun, we were warned of the dangerous conditions ahead. It was drizzling, foggy, overcast, and the road was slick. At the start of the Boston Marathon is a steep downhill. The race officials told us in no uncertain terms to brake going down the hill and be very cautious.

Of course, the guys in the front row are thinking, "Let's get out of here fast and away from the rest of the chairs." The second row isn't going to hold back if the first row doesn't, so the warning of caution went unheeded by everyone. Boom! The starting gun goes off. In just a few seconds we were going

30 m.p.h., crowded together, with chairs swerving in and out. Although somewhat dangerous in dry weather, the drizzle made it treacherous.

In just a short time, one of the wheelers in front lost control of his chair and started sliding across the road in front of the other wheelers. It was a moment of panic and chairs were flying everywhere. Some wheelers were literally upside down sliding down the road, while others were smashing into the curb and other wheelchairs. Pat Holly, from Oregon, instantly came sliding across in front of me.

My heart jumped into my throat and I swerved to the left, up on two wheels, and was ready for my appointment with the concrete.

In the next second, I had somehow gone around Pat and was back down on four wheels! Tony Possehl was behind me, and he wasn't so fortunate. (Yes, this is the same Tony that had the heart attack a year later, 20 miles down the road on Heartbreak Hill.) His chair flipped up, went swerving down the road, and skidded off until he hit the curb.

Several racers were seriously injured and didn't get back in the race. Tony, however, wasn't seriously hurt and fixed his tire, straightened his chair, and got back on the road again. I think several photographers sensed the crash was going to happen, because they were right on the scene when it happened and perfect pictures of the crash were taken. The Boston Globe newspaper entitled the accompanying article, "Wheels of Misfortune" and Tony got his picture in the paper twice.

As a result of the crashes, there were rule changes in 1988: 1) Everyone must wear helmets and, 2) The police car will pace you down the hill with your brakes on. Anyone who passes the police car is disqualified. The race will start at the bottom of the hill. No problem!

9

IRONWOOD SPRINGS CHRISTIAN RANCH

"If you want to stay young, work with young people, if you want to die young, try and keep up with them."   —Copied

Ironwood Springs Christian Ranch started in May 1976. It is a non-profit, non-denominational, year around youth and family camp. It is located along the Root River in southeastern Minnesota on 200 acres of woods, with trails and wildlife. We serve 16,000 people annually.

It had been seven years since I left Colorado with a dream to start a youth camp. Seven years of regular frustration in this goal, leading me to often think I was spinning my wheels.

During this seven years which led up to my accident, I had worked in Caterpillar construction, finished college and seminary, married, traveled in Europe and the Mid-East for six months, and taught school. Now, being confined to a wheelchair, could my dream of camp work ever come true? If you're like me, waiting seven minutes is difficult, much less seven years.

We all want pat answers to hard questions. Where am I

going? How do I get there? What is it going to cost? Instead of answers, I had no idea what my future held.

In 1971, two years before my injury, dad and I took a hike along the Root River where we heard a large spring gushing cool, refreshing water. We walked through the beautiful rolling hills covered with Oak, Maple, Poplar, Ironwood, and Black Walnut trees. The spring was about a half mile from the road, and when we got there, we couldn't believe how beautiful it was. Was this the place to start a camp? We wondered who owned the land and if they would be interested in selling.

> We had looked all around the tri-state area for property for several years, and could it be that here 'under our feet,' where we had lived most of our life, was the property that God had in mind for the camp?

Excited, we found out the farmer who owned the land: Roger. We offered him $350 an acre for 40 acres. Well, Roger just didn't seem nearly as excited as we did about the proposition to sell his woods.

We asked him to call us if he ever changed his mind.

Six months later, the call came (ya-hoo!) from Roger. "Are you still interested in buying that land?" asked Roger. "Yes we are," I anxiously answered. "How does $250 an acre sound?" Speechless for a moment, I finally said, "Yes, we will be right out."

We bought the 40 acres in 1971 and the dream began.

WHAT'S IN A NAME?

IRONWOOD - The woods were filled with Ironwood (Hop Hornbeam) trees. They are small, very hard, usually in a cluster of two or three, and have a bud on them the whitetail deer seem to like. If you have any intention of driving a nail through an Ironwood, forget it.

SPRINGS - The spring became the focus of the camp where

we would build our first building. It has a capacity of approximately 100 gallons of water per minute, and is the most cool and refreshing water you can find.

CHRISTIAN - We wanted to provide an atmosphere and opportunity for people to get to know God, themselves, and others better. Leading people to a personal relationship with Jesus Christ as Lord and Savior is our ultimate goal. We teach self-esteem and want to promote making new friends as part of our Christian message.

RANCH - I wanted to have a western setting with horses, horse equipment, animals, fences and buildings that would be ranch style. This desire came from my experience in Colorado.

1971-1975

We built a lodge first, got a dozen or so horses, hosted a summer camp or two, but all that time we seemed to lack vision. I was still in school, working on my first master's degree, and with any extra time I had, I worked for dad in construction. During this time we developed many trails, built a nice driveway, made an athletic field and shaped a snow tubing hill.

When I had my accident in 1973, dad felt we should put the property up for sale and make a nice profit. I didn't know what to think. I was vulnerable, being unsure of my future abilities. I believed my faith was strong enough to see me through, but being uncertain of what to do, I told dad, "It's your property; your life's investment. You make the decision." The land was on the market for six months. Many people expressed interest and from any human standpoint, it should have been sold.

GOD HAD ANOTHER PLAN

After the six months and my three month stay in the hospital ended, dad asked me if I still wanted to have the camp, get it organized, establish a purpose, and make it a non-profit camp. My reply was "Yes, but it's your property and your life's investment. Besides I don't have any idea what I can do strapped to a wheelchair the rest of my life."

Dad's reply was, "I'll give you three months to make your decision if you want to start the camp."

For the next three months I followed the wisdom of Solomon in Proverbs 15:22, "Plans fail for lack of counsel, but with many advisors they succeed."

I spent the next three months brainstorming, praying, talking with friends, neighbors, pastors, other camp folks, farmers, college buddies and anyone else willing to give me input. It turned out to be an encourageing and supportive time. "Tell me when and where you want your first (organizational) meeting, and I'll be there," was the comment of many interested people.

May 22, 1976 was our first meeting. This was an organizational time to establish our purpose, elect our board, and begin the task of drawing up the by-laws, articles of incorporation, and other legal matters. It took approximately four years to get all the legal work done to become an independent non-profit 501-C3 charity.

Ironwood has become a tribute to God and our community. The camp was given its legal beginning in 1976 with 40 acres, two horses, one employee, and our first week of camp. We have continued to grow each year. It's God's camp, so we ask for His wisdom each day to be the good stewards he wants us to be. Literally hundreds of people each year get involved in supporting the camp.

WHO DO WE SERVE?

We serve families and community groups such as: schools, scouts, churches, 4-H, senior citizens, groups working with the disabled, service clubs, several local and county/regional agencies, and host birthday parties, weddings, and business functions.

HOW ARE WE FUNDED?

Seventy-five percent of our funding comes from camper fees. The remaining 25 percent comes from a variety of fundraisers. We have a benefit auction in the Spring where over 400 businesses and individuals get involved by donating items to be sold at the auction. Other fundraising events include a mid-February pancake benefit supper, and the outdoor sportmans weekend in September.

Other sources include service clubs, individuals, special grants, civic groups, churches, corporations, businesses and foundations.

SPECIAL EVENTS

Our special events during the year include: a teen snow camp, Memorial Day Open House, lumberjack weekend, a quilters' camp weekend, Outdoor Sportsmans Retreat, and an appreciation dinner ending the year.

VOLUNTEERS

Ironwood is blessed in that it has 150-200 volunteers each year who put in over 2,000 hours. Without their generous giving and support, the camp would have never reached the point where it is at today. Besides their work, they provide that encouragement that keeps us going.

STAFF

Our fulltime staff has grown to eight, with approximately 30 additional staff in the summer. The staff is what really makes the biggest difference in the campers' lives. We have been richly blessed with a dedicated staff who all work hard to accomplish our mission. I am grateful to each of them for using their God-given talents to serve others. Our current employees include: Dan Ostergard, George and Carol Wyland, Mary Ann Schultz, and Ernie, Jan and Ginny Gafkjen.

BOARD OF DIRECTORS

Our volunteer Board of Directors meet monthly and they include: Bob Bardwell, Lester Bardwell, Eleanor Crane, Rusty Fiek, Gary Froiland, Dr. Robert Jensen, David Koehler, Dan Ostergard, John Regehr, Clay Ruggles, and Joe Stanich. Their service and committment to the camp is really appreciated.

IRONWOOD TODAY

— Two hundred acres; thirty horses; swimming pool; tennis courts; recreation center; minifarm

— Main lodge; dining hall, seating 125

— log chapel seating 250

— Cabins with sleeping space for approximately one hundred and fifty people

— Trail riding, fifty camp sites for tents and RV's; superslide; paddle boats on the river

— Winter activities including snowtubing hill with 80 tubes and a tow rope, cross country skiing, sleigh rides.

SUMMER CAMPING PROGRAMS

We have eight weeks of camp in the summer for kids. We start with second graders. We have speciality Horse n' Trail camps called "trailblazers," "ranchhands," and "highriders." Rod "Lucky" Everding and Teri Laschkewitsch join us in the summer months for our horsemanship programs. There are also various levels of camp for junior high and high school students. These are all week-long camps from Monday through Friday.

This special camp got started in 1986 to provide a place for the physically challenged to come from across the country and participate in several different sporting events. This past summer we had six different disabilities represented. Seventy-five kids and adults came from 15 states. We have participation in: road racing, tennis, horseback riding, water skiing, bowling, paintball games, swimming, softball, basketball, and table sports. The camp is the third week of July each year. Each year we are privileged to have world class people, some athletes and some not, who come and share their inspiring lives and tell how they have turned their disability into something positive. They also get involved in teaching and demonstrating the different sports.

Some of those include: Jim Martinson, co-director of the camp and Olympic road racer and downhill skier from Washington; Scot Hollonbeck, top American and Olympic road racer from Atlanta; Jean Driscoll, seven-time Boston Marathon winner and an Olympian; Bob Weiland, national motivational speaker and athlete from California who, as a double amputee, walked across America using his arms; Kevin Saunders, Olympian in the pentathalon from Alabama; W. Mitchell, national motivational speaker from Colorado; and Karl Kassulke, twelve year player with the Minnesota Vikings.

The theme: Disabled Don't Disqualify!

I did just what you said Mr Bob, I brought a friend to camp.

S.O.A.R. (Spiritual Outdoor Adventure Retreats)

These are off-site, co-ed camps for ages 12-17 that are divided into three phases. Phase One: This is for ages 12-14 and, as a first-year camp, is based at Ironwood. The goal is for the campers to learn outdoor skills and a variety of sporting activities such as canoeing, rope climbing, biking, and horseback riding.

<u>Phase Two:</u> This is for ages 14-15 and is for those who met the requirement to go to the boundary waters for five days of canoeing in Northern Minnesota.

<u>Phase Three:</u> This is for ages 16-17 and goes to Horn Creek Ranch (the camp I worked at during college) in Westcliffe, Colorado for mountain climbing, whitewater rafting, and horseback riding.

OUR MESSAGE

Beside the message of salvation for all youth, we have different themes each year. Some of the important issues we cover with teens are dating and morality. We use the "true love waits" campaign theme to address peer pressure and issues our teens face today (addictions from substance abuse, pornography, sexually transmitted diseases, etc.) that are destroying the fabric of this country's youth.

We remind the youth that God does have a few "house rules" in this world and whether we choose to follow them or not, we are accountable, just as the law of gravity. The "law of the harvest" applies to our lives as well as the farmer. God says in Galatians 6:9 "What you sow, you reap." Two rules to remember about this law: 1) The harvest is always in the future and 2) Your harvest is according to what you have sown.

We encourage young people to set up some unshakeable-unbreakables, "no passing zones" in their lives that they will not allow to be compromised or violated, and to build the foundation of their life on honesty, integrity, morality, decency, courage and godliness so when the storms of life come crashing down, they can be strong.

> Everyone is reminded that, regardless of bad experiences or mistakes in the past, we have a Father in heaven who is loving and forgiving.

In a day of confused identities, distorted priorities, and negotiable values, it's good to know there are some absolutes. It's time to sound the alarm in our communities and speak up for the values upon which this great country was founded.

IRONWOOD ADVENTURES FROM A WHEELERS PERSPECTIVE

I was riding my lawntractor with a snowplow, going down our driveway pushing the snow off the road. I hit a bump, which flipped my right leg off the platform and it landed in front of the tire. I wasn't watching this incident, and before I knew it the chain on the wheel caught the top of my boot and it pulled nearly my entire leg under the wheel. I finally got the tractor stopped, put it in reverse, and backed off my leg. I lifted up my leg and noticed my ankle and foot drop. I knew I had a broken ankle.

I drove home and got in my car and drove to the hospital, emergency entrance. Not feeling the pain, the doctor set my broken ankle bone, put it in a cast up to the knee and sent me back to my hospital room. In a short time an orderly returned and said the doctor did not like the x-ray of the ankle and that it needed to be redone. As I came back to the exam room, the man who put on my cast asked, "What are you doing back here?"

"Didn't you hear the bad news?" I replied.

"No, what?" he said as he tilted his head in question.

"You put the cast on the wrong leg." I answered. After his surprised and worried look, I told him I was joking. He reset the ankle bone, put on a new cast, and sent me back to my room. I went home the next day. At a return visit, they told me it's healed, but to be honest, it felt just fine before!

HIGH WATER

I have a six-wheel ATV that has floatation ability that I often use to cross the Root River that flows through the camp. I had taken the drain plugs out, so when crossing the river, I knew I had to move quickly (no problem). The current was a bit stronger than I had thought and was pulling me downstream, making it a challenge to get to the other side of the river. Before

long the water had come in the drain plug holes and had gotten on the drive belt which threw water on the spark plug. You guessed it. I gurgled to the bottom (about three feet) and of course was stranded. After about three hours of watching the birds and seeing the sun come closer and closer to the horizon, there was a small glimmer of hope. Coming from a distant bank, I could make out the sound of voices. I called out and Wes, one of our employees, came down and saw my predicament. I learned another lesson in the school of life and decided to have a CB installed.

MY BROTHER

I had driven up to our maintenance shop in my four-wheel mule, which is somewhat like a golf cart. A man came out who was doing volunteer work at the ranch, and asked me if I knew the guy in a wheelchair who runs the camp. "I think his name is Bob," he said. I told him, "Yes, he looks a lot like me – we've even been called brothers. He's a real friendly guy. He should be in for noon lunch, so you can meet him then." He was sitting at a table in the dining hall with a group of other guys when I rolled up and asked, "Have you had a chance to meet Bob yet?" After a moment of confusion, we all had a big laugh.

THE SLEIGH RIDE THAT WASN'T

I was driving a team of Belgian horses, giving a sleigh ride to a group of people around horseshoe trail on our back forty acres. All was going well until a pin on the bobsled broke. I was catapolted into the air and after I slammed to the ground was being dragged through the woods by a team of runaway horses. I let go of the line and the horses continued their runaway. The people on the sleigh came running up to see if I was still alive. Of course, they didn't know I was paralyzed.

You should have seen the look on their faces when I told them that I couldn't get up, and that I thought I was paralyzed. I soon confessed!

They picked me up and carried me to a snowmobile. The horses continued at full gallop until their first turn. Instead of turning, they went straight ahead into the trees and were soon stuck in the brush, unable to go further. Thus, the sleigh ride ended and the people all walked home with a Christmas memory.

10

VICTORY IN DEFEAT

"Some goals are so high and lofty, that to fall short of reaching them, is still cause for a CELEBRATION."
—Bob Bardwell

The stories in this chapter have left me with some of the best memories of my life.

The first time I dreamed of making the Olympic team was in freestyle wrestling. As I told earlier, Jim and Dave Hazewinkel, whom I met during my senior year in Bible college, mentored me in freestyle wrestling.

My 1972 Olympic hopes ended when I dislocated my right knee in the Olympic trials in Coon Rapids, Minnesota, ending my 10-year wrestling career. About this time, I came across the following article written by Cliff Cushman, a great hurdler for the University of Kansas who also competed in the Olympic trials. He wrote this letter to his former high school friends because he had received so many letters from them telling how sorry they were that he knocked down a hurdle and did not qualify for the Olympics. Later Cliff was missing in action in Vietnam.

YOU DON'T KNOW UNTIL YOU'VE TRIED...
A challenge to youth

Don't feel sorry for me. I feel sorry for some of you. You may have seen the U.S. Olympic trials on television. If so, you watched me hit the fifth hurdle, fall, and lie on the track in an inglorious heap of skinned elbows, bruised hips, torn knees, and injured pride, unsuccessful in my attempt to make the Olympic team for the second time. In a split second, all the many years of training, pain, sweat, blisters, and agony of running were simply and irrevocably wiped out. But I tried! I would much rather fall knowing I had put forth an honest effort than never to have tried at all.

Everyone has own "Olympic team"

This is not to say that everyone is capable of making the Olympic Team. However, each of you is capable of trying to make your own personal "Olympic Team", whether it be the high school athletic team, the glee club, the honor roll, or whatever your goal may be. Unless your reach exceeds your grasp, how can you be sure what you can attain. Don't you think there are things better than cigarettes, hot rod cars, school drop outs, excessive make-up and grease cuts?

Over 15 years ago, I saw a star - first place in the Olympic Games. I literally started to run after it. In 1960 I came within three yards of grabbing it; this year I stumbled, fell and watched it recede four more years away. Certainly, I was very disappointed in falling flat on my face. However, there is nothing I can do about it now, but go pick the cinders from my wounds and take one more step followed by one more and one more, until the steps turn into miles and the miles into success. I know I may never make it. The odds are against me, but I have something in my favor - desire and faith. Romans 5:3-5 has always had an inspirational meaning to me in this regard. "...we rejoice in our sufferings, knowing that suffering produces endurance, and endurance produces character, and character produces hope, and hope does not disappoint us..." At least I am going to try.

How about you? Would a little extra effort on your part bring up your grade average? Would you have a better chance to make the athletic team if you stayed an extra 15 minutes after practice and worked on your moves?

Let me tell you something about yourselves. You are taller and heavier than any past generation in this country, you are spending more money, enjoying more freedom, and driving more cars than ever before, yet many of you are very unhappy. Some of you have never known the satisfaction of doing your best in sports, the joy of excelling in class, the wonderful feeling of completing a job, any job, and looking back on it knowing that you have done your best.

I Dare You to Reach for the Stars

I dare you to have your hair cut and not wilt under the comments of your so-called friends. I dare you to clean up your language. I dare you to honor your mother and father. I dare you to go to church without having to be compelled to go by your parents. I dare you to unselfishly help someone less fortunate than yourself and enjoy the wonderful feeling that goes with it. I dare you to become physically fit. I dare you to read a book that is not required in school. I dare you to look up at the stars not down at the mud and set your sights on one of them that, up to now, you thought was unattainable. There's plenty of room at the top but no room for anyone to sit down.

Who knows? You may be surprised at what you can achieve with sincere effort. So get up, pick the cinders out of your wounds and take one more step. I DARE YOU!"

My wheelchair road racing career began in 1983 and by 1988 I felt I had a shot at making the Paralympic marathon team. In six years I had put approximately 6,500 miles on my wheelchair, completed 25 marathons, and gained considerable experience on the world class circuit in 1987. I believed that 1988 was to be the peak in my racing career.

Invacare, a wheelchair company, put together for the first time the *Invacare Cup Racing Series*. The requirement to compete in the cup series was that five out of seven different races throughout the country must be completed. My friend and racing buddy, Tony Possehl, and I signed up for the series and competed in the Seattle, Phoenix, Tampa, Atlanta, Los Angeles and Long Beach races.

DISAPPOINTMENT STRIKES

I had a disappointing race at the Peachtree, in Atlanta, Georgia. One of my racing goals was to complete a 10K in less than 30 minutes. As we raced, we watched our computers and the mile markers and knew we had a good chance at a sub-30 finish. The last quarter of a mile of the race is in a park with a steep hill and a sharp left at the bottom. Coming into the curve along with Tony and a dozen other wheelers, I lost concentration with the excitement and the noise of the crowd and went up on two wheels. I tried screeching the brakes, but I hit the curb.

There was a row of three-foot telephone poles about 24 inches apart and five feet back from the curb to keep people out of the park and warn them of the dangerous curve. Airborne, I flew between the telephone poles, smashing my left front corner and sheering off the left push rim. I landed upside down under an

evergreen tree listening to the birds, I mean bells, ringing in my head. I was out of the race. I was disappointed, but glad to be alive.

Tony and I ended our racing year at the Long Beach half-marathon. I finished the cup series in 16th place and Tony was 17th.

Although it was the end of the year, my mind was already on the 1988 Los Angeles Marathon in March. This was an important race because I knew the top ten finishers would be selected to go on in an effort to qualify for the marathon in the fall Paralympics in Seoul, Korea.

LOS ANGELES MARATHON 1

Being from Minnesota, the months before March are not ideal for training for a marathon. The slick roads and deep snow drifts to break through, as well as the discomfort of frostbitten fingers and difficulty sucking up the ice in my water bottle, forced creativity.

I made a set of training rollers in my basement and everyday, starting in January, I trained hard in anticipation of the marathon on the third of March.

Some of the perks for wheelchair athletes include transporation from the airport to the hotel, hotel accommodations, and a lift to the starting line. I arrived in Los Angeles early on March 2nd and by early that evening, 125 wheelers had been transported from the airport to their hotel. Almost every athlete has two wheelchairs, their everyday chair and their racing chair, totaling 250 chairs – that was the easy part.

The race directors announced a 7:00 p.m. meeting to give important instructions for the bus ride early the next morning. The race time was 8:00 a.m. and we were told to be down in the lobby of the hotel no later than 5:30 a.m. in order to get to the Los Angeles Coliseum on time. That night I shared a room with Tim O'Connell from Alaska, who ended up placing second in the race. With thoughts of the 125 wheelers and 15,000 runners competing in the race, I went to bed with a bit of a stomach ache. I woke the next morning with excitement, ready for the challenge.

NO PROBLEM

Most of us were sitting out at the lobby entrance at 5:30 the next morning. Our chairs were fine-tuned and laps stacked with tire pumps, water bottles, tape, gloves, racing numbers, and a few tools. At 6:00 a.m. there were still no buses. We were getting a bit nervous. About 15 minutes later three old city buses pulled up and announced they were to pick up the wheelers. (Have you seen the old yellow LA buses? They're tough enough to get on if you're able bodied.) Don't worry about it, I thought, it's the same for everyone.

Tim O'Connell, sitting next to me said, "I wonder where we put our racing chairs?" Right then they announced, "Come on, let's get the chairs loaded in these compartments." as they lifted the storage doors. To their amazement, the chairs would not fit. Panic time.

We concluded that whoever was assigned to getting the buses just wasn't 'the sharpest knife in the drawer.' "All right, everyone must take off your rear wheels from your racers and we'll load them (rear wheels) inside the bus." they announced. And they did. They stacked our rear wheels in the back of the bus to the ceiling.

The wheelers were already upset that the buses were late and by this time there were some boiling hot radiators (or wheelers). This was a very important race to so many of us and we were ready to tell the race committee to go and *gargle with nine yards of concrete.*

Already we were going to be late to the starting line and a new mass of confusion erupted when they tried to get us into the bus. Finally, by a two-man lift, we were carried out of our chairs and into the bus as our wheels were being stacked in the rear.

I was one of the lucky ones and got dropped in the seat behind the driver. I would be the first one off. We pulled into the parking lot with 30 minutes until race time.

Once again, another dilemma – they couldn't carry us off the buses and set us on the blacktop; our back porches don't do asphalt parking lots!

Volunteers were being summoned to help unload our everyday chairs from the vans so when we got unloaded from the bus, we could sit in someone else's chair. That wasn't so bad, as long as we didn't have to *race* in someone else's chair.

WHERE'S MY CHAIR?

Then came the tricky part - finding my racing wheels out of

a selection of about 250. Of course, only the owner can identify his wheels. About the time I located my racing chair and wheels I heard over the loud speakers, "Ten minutes until the start of the wheelchair race." About half of us were ready when someone announced, "Follow me to the start of the race." I'll never forget, I looked back and there was one of the elite racers, Laverne Achenbach, still on the bus, waving his arms out the window pleading for someone to help.

Soon after we began rolling to the starting line, I heard our guide say, "Oh, how do you get through there?" As we came up against a yellow fence. The cops quickly came over, pulled the posts out of the ground, and lifted the fence. We all made it under, but time was running out and there were still two more fences between us and the starting line.

THE STARTING GUN GOES OFF

By now, Laverne had made it off the bus and most of us were lined up at the starting line awaiting the gun. Although only getting a 60-second warm up instead of the normal two-to-three miles of road work, I was feeling pumped. Four miles into the race, I was in the second pack of racers – approximately 25th place. About that time on my right, Bill Fricke from Long Beach went pushing by with his head down. "That guy is going places," I thought to myself. So I got behind Bill, and wow, did we cruise! I don't know how many chairs we reeled in, but Bill and I had places to go and people to catch.

Not too often can you catch the lead pack, but at mile 21 we pulled into their draft. I couldn't believe it, I was in the top 10 and on my way to the best race in my career. With less than a mile from the finish line, I started feeling queasy with my energy level flashing on empty. I rolled across the finish line in seventh place overall, the third American, and only one minute off the first-place time.

CELEBRATION TIME

With having made the top ten, Olympic dreams ran vividly

through my mind. I soon discovered the level of competition I had to maintain and the commitments I had to make throughout the summer months, and I knew I had to make some choices. To continue would mean sacrificing time as director of our summer youth camp, and I decided not to continue Paralympic pursuits. Regardless, the memories and accomplishments of the race will be mine forever.

ON THE SIDE...

By the way, Los Angeles Marathon II transported the wheelers to hotels near the start of the race and from there, we wheeled to the starting line. Laverne preferred this arrangement!

I've been back to the Los Angeles marathon four different times and have experienced it at a first class level. It takes time to get the bugs out of anything worthwhile.

11

GRACE HAPPENS

Stronger Than Before
Even though the rain comes down,
It brings life into the ground,
And I know the sun will shine,
That brings hope again to this heart of mine.
I know that God will heal all things,
Broken lives and broken wings.
Only He can mend the hearts,
That this world has tore apart.
As the seasons make their turn,
There's a lesson here to learn,
Broken wings take time to mend,
Before they learn to fly again.
On the breath of God I'll soar,
I'll be STRONGER THAN BEFORE.
Don't look back into the past,
What was fire now is ash,
Let it all be dead and gone,
Time is now for movin' on, for movin' on.
*Bill and Janny Grein

I find music to be a great spirit lifter and mender and hearing the words of this song gave me hope and encouragement during some of the lowest times of failure in my life.

*Used with permission "Mighty Wind Music", P.O. Box 2637, Plant City, FL 33564

I credit the phrase "Grace Happens" to my pastor and friend, John Morris. We were discussing some of the circumstances and sin in my life and how God has turned so many scars into stars for me, and Pastor John's comment was "Grace Happens."

I was married in the summer of 1972 to Marilyn, a gal I had known in high school. Six years after high school we started dating, at which time I had one year left to get my Master's Degree. I had just returned from my four months of travel in Europe and Israel.

I was eager to get married; most of my friends were and I felt like all the girls may be gone soon, so Marilyn seemed a good choice. She was a Christian and had just graduated from another Bible College. We were engaged, made plans to marry, and all went smooth (on the outside at least) until the wedding.

We had very little counsel; after all, we seemed like such a nice match. I had been having a strange stomach ache (later I found out Marilyn did, as well) for some time and felt I wanted out of this relationship, but saw no way of turning back now. There was certainly nothing wrong with Marilyn, but I just didn't have the inner excitement and peace that I thought should accompany this big decision.

But for all I knew, everyone had these feelings before their wedding. Well, the wedding day was June 10, 1972. I ignored my stomach ache, and we were off to the honeymoon. Then it was back to construction work to finish the summer and back to seminary to wrap up my post-graduate work.

For almost 12 years we struggled in this relationship, which seemed to never bond. We certainly had some fun times together, but never seemed to be strengthening our relationship. And thus it sat stagnant for most of the time. I just didn't know what to do.

One year after our marriage I became paralyzed through my construction accident. It would have been easy to blame the broken relationship on my injury. (Just think of the adjustments that a spouse has to go through when their mate has their life altered so dramatically!)

90

> I knew blaming others or the environment wasn't right and that I needed to look inside to see where I failed to find the *true* solution.

Our marriage only just survived for all those years. I say this much to my shame. I felt responsible and trapped at the same time. If I had heard one message or talk about marriage, I had heard hundreds. Many messages were on saving the marriage and bringing about reconciliation, which is always God's first and best plan. Then, I heard messages on those who have already had a relationship end in divorce and how "Grace happened" in their lives.

I was continually caught in the web of wanting to obey God and yet wanting out of this marriage. We attended counseling sessions, a marriage encounter weekend, and still the bond didn't seem to develop.

I felt that breaking the marriage vow was probably the greatest of sins and that my life would have little purpose for the Lord if this marriage ended in divorce.

I was reminded that there is a big difference between failing and being a failure.

Failing to me is being human and making mistakes. Yes, some will be costly for a lifetime, while others you learn from and go on. I remember reading an article titled, "Failure, The Backdoor to Success."

START OVER

When you've made your plans and they've gone awry,
When you've tried your best 'til there's no more try,
When you've failed yourself and you don't know why
Start over.
When you've prayed to God so you'll know His will,
When you've prayed and prayed but you don't know still,
When you want to stop 'cause you've had your fill
Start over.

When the year's been long and successes few,
When December comes and you're feeling blue,
God gives a January just so you
Start over.
Starting over means victories won,
Starting over means a race well run,
Starting over means the Lord's "Well done,"
...so don't just sit there, START OVER.

* Woodrow Kroll

Finally, after almost 12 years, I felt I was being a bigger hypocrite and sinner by staying in an empty relationship than by admitting my failure and sin, getting out, and starting over.

I didn't know how friends and people would react to my divorce. I felt very vulnerable and low in spirit. Yes, I could have stayed in the unbonded relationship another 12 years, but the pain, along with having only one life to live, motivated me to get a divorce.

If going through with the divorce would have created bitterness, anger, and an unworkable plan, I would have not gone ahead with it. We had no children (we had started the adoption process once and backed out because of our unstable relationship). To me, there is no such thing as divorce when children are involved. In camp work, I often see the aftermath of bitterness, resentment, anger, unforgiveness, and the lifetime of scars when children are involved in divorce situations. I know "Grace happens" here too.

We agreed on the terms of our divorce and I felt I had no unfinished business, so the marriage ended one year later.

What happens when one who calls himself a Christian gets a divorce? Several things happened to me: 1) I felt I had let God down – His plan is reconciliation; 2) I felt future service for the Lord was tarnished, and; 3) I wondered if I would get a second chance for marriage.

*Used with permission "Back to the Bible Broadcast", Lincoln, Nebraska

GOOD NEWS

Following the divorce the popular song, "Stronger Than Before", already mentioned, and some of the lyrics of another song, "I'm not lookin' behind me at mistakes I've already made..." gave me renewed strength.

I felt strong support from many of my true friends and got several letters of encouragement and Christian love. There were also those who pulled away and couldn't support me or the Christian camp. That was okay with me for those who felt uncomfortable about my choice. I understand. I realized that nothing can separate us from the love of Christ.

I haven't changed my opinion on what God says about divorce. God was the creator of man and marriage was His plan for us.

God intended marriage to be permanent, life-long and said that those who honor it will be blessed, fulfilled, and experience the greatest joys of the human heart.

Within a year a single gal named Jode Fox brought a group of kids from Junior Achievement out to Ironwood for a sleigh ride, and a seemingly chance business encounter turned into a lifetime together. We dated for several years before marrying on May 11, 1991.

The relationship had a lot of hurdles to clear, bridges to build, and prayers to be answered before marriage could happen. She is 14 years younger than me, our religious backgrounds are different, and it often looked as though this would only be a friendship.

I believe it was "Grace happening" when on February 14, 1991, I asked her to marry me. I had invited her out to the house that evening with plans of going out for supper. Instead we got in my six-wheel ATV and drove out to my favorite spot along the Root River. It was after dark and I had a gallon can with holes punched in it that read, "Will you marry me?" She was blindfolded while I was lighting the candle inside the can. When she took off the blindfold and saw the words, "Will you marry me?" She gave me the biggest hug and kiss, hesitated a moment, but said, "Yes." On the way back to the house in 30-degree below zero wind chill and storm warnings out, we got stuck in the snow and she had to push us out!

We arrived back home, and I had planned to take her out for dinner at the Anderson House in Wabasha, Minnesota. Her favorite jeweler had a shop in Wabasha and I had secretly arranged for the owner, Rueben, to meet us after hours to pick out a ring.

As we were driving down main street in Wabasha heading for the Anderson House we drove past the jewelry store. I said, "Look, Jode, the jewelry store looks like it still might be open – the lights are on. Should we stop and check the door?" "No way," Jode said. I turned around and pulled up in front of the store. Jode got out, walked over, and pulled on the door. Wow, it opened. She hollered in and Rueben, from the back of the store, said, "Come on in." Jode just couldn't believe that Rueben happened to work late that night. (Ha!) For the next two hours we looked and talked and finally picked out a ring. Just before we left, I thought I should call the Anderson House and see if we still had our reservations. Much to my dismay, they were closed for the night due to the weather. Plan B was to go to the only other open place for food which was Kwik Trip, a gas and munchies stop. We had apple juice and a warmed-up pizza to close out the evening. We are now in our seventh year of marriage and I have felt bonded and truly love Jode.

The words "trust" and "commitment" have real meaning and I am grateful beyond words for God's grace in my life. I have experienced first-hand God's forgiveness and grace in allowing me to have a second chance.

Amy Grant sings, "If you've found someone who's tender, if

you've found someone's who true, thank the Lord, He's been DOUBLY GOOD to you."

I believe I am worthy of God's love and forgiveness, because He made me and has a purpose for my life. I have experienced the abundant blessings of the Lord and have a marriage relationship that means the world to me.

Marriage takes work. What is worthwhile and lasting that doesn't take work? There are no weedless gardens without work, no shiny shoes without polish and no healthy thriving marriages without effort and commitment each day.

Is there a guarantee this marriage will last? No. But it will last by God's grace because I want it to and will make the daily commitment and effort to see our relationship not only survive, but flourish and grow stronger each day. I can't explain how one can go through with a divorce, remarry, and live an abundant life, other than "Grace happens."

"Grace"—that word to me means that God gives us far beyond what we are worthy of or ever can dream or expect. Why does He? Because He is God and He loves us unconditionally. I encourage you to give Him a chance in your life if you haven't already. 'Grace' will happen to you too, and you will be overwhelmed by what He can do.

In His Time

In His time, in His time
He makes all things beautiful in His time.
Lord please show me every day,
As you're teaching me your way,
That you do just what you say, in Your time.

*Diane Ball

*Used with permission "Maranatha Music"

IRONWOOD SPRINGS CHRISTIAN RANCH

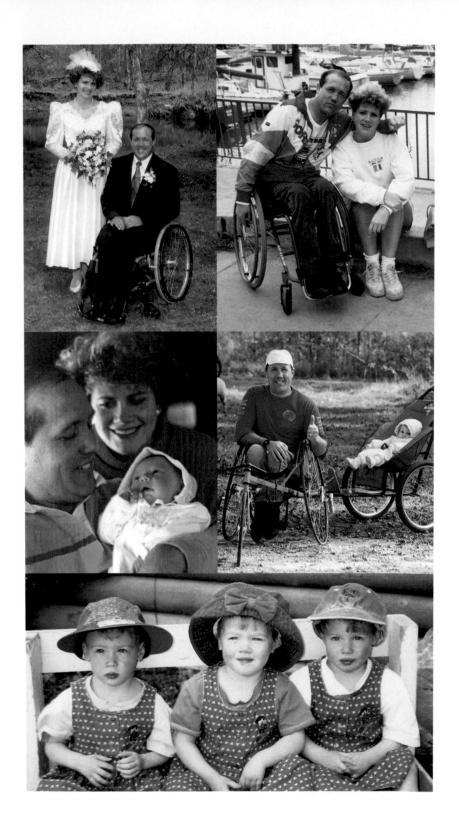

12

JODE'S JOURNEY

by Jode Bardwell

It was an odd premonition. Totally out of place.

I was trolloping through the woods at Ironwood Springs Christian Ranch on my first visit there, what was supposed to be a brief, routine, business visit. I came upon a beautiful log home. Suddenly and briefly I was overcome with the feeling that someday I would live in that home.

How strange. I wasn't in the market for a log home. The feeling, although strong, made no sense and passed quickly.

But I *would* live there. My visit to Ironwood Springs marked the beginning of my life with Bob Bardwell.

I was coordinator of our local Junior Achievement chapter in 1987. As a special outing, we decided to take the teens to Ironwood for a horse drawn sleigh ride just before Christmas. I hadn't heard of Ironwood, but on a referral I called, scheduled, and got directions for our outing.

After the outing, I went into the office to pay and that's where I first encountered Bob. I thought it weird that a very handsome man like this wouldn't be home with his family. We chatted, I paid with a check that had my phone number printed on it, and as I said my good-byes I thought, "He seems like an intelligent type. If he's interested in contacting me, he'll surely take my phone number from the check."

For a year I thought I must have been flattering myself because I never heard from him. Then, unexpectedly, I bumped into him at a basketball game. It 'just so happened' that on my to-do list was scheduling a sleigh ride for my department at IBM. I re-introduced myself to Bob and told him I'd call him in the morning to schedule the ride. I wouldn't say it looked like a bolt of lightening had hit him or even that a light bulb had come on, but the next day he did ask me to a basketball game that was to be played just after Christmas.

We've had a wonderful eight years since that first date. I believe I've done more in these years than I thought I'd do the rest of my life.

After my first date with Bob, I realized the source of many of his struggles and frustrations. He was still dealing with the scars and healing of a divorce.

Bob and I dated for a little more than two years before marrying. Some of those days were heavenly, others seemed devastating. Bob and I have a number of big differences in background and personality.

> — I am less of a risk taker, one who needs more security, while Bob is more 'fun.'
> — Bob loves a crowd. I prefer close friends.
> — Bob cheers our girls on as they climb over tall objects. I call to them to be careful.

However, our personalities complement each other more than not. I often go along to his speaking engagements to be an encouragement. I admire his depth of character and his tireless listening ear (even if it makes him late for dinner appointments with me!)

We differ in material priorities. I would give my eye teeth for air conditioning on those smoldering summer days. He wants a '65 Mustang.

Bob was 40 and I was 26 when we met. As we dated and contemplated marriage, we saw many different hurdles. He had a failed marriage and wasn't so sure he wanted the struggles I could potentially bring. (He says I'm stubborn!) I wasn't as afraid of Bob's physical disability as I was of all the compromises our marital relationship entailed.

I was fine from a financial standpoint and kept busy enough socially.

I desired children, as my family was my most precious earthly treasure. In considering marriage to Bob, I felt assured that if we did decide to marry, God would provide children. We were both very open to adoption as a beautiful way of building a family. Even now, after we've been abundantly blessed biologically, we talk about adopting in coming years.

> I looked at Bob's wheelchair and saw it as his handicap. I soon realized though that every marriage will have a handicap, some are just visible, while others are not, i.e., alcoholism, abuse, workaholism just to name a few.

I felt I could deal with this known disability, although there are days I get very frustrated with loading his chair in the van or doing the majority of the hauling, be it groceries or babies.

Bob's proposal came at a time when I was ready to give up. My mother had just been diagnosed with cancer and I felt my world was falling apart. I was frustrated with his lack of commitment and I was ready to move on but just as I wondered if he would ever get serious, he proposed.

He proposed on Valentines Day of 1991 and we were married down by the river in May of that same year. Within sight of the spring house at Ironwood Springs, the ceremony took place with a canopy of leaves overhead and the greening trees alongside the narrow, calm river as a backdrop. The weather was perfect. There was a slight slope down to the river which gave our 100-or-so guests a beautiful view of the ceremony.

> A more perfect cathedral could never be found than that which is chiseled by the hand of God. I remember thinking the day was passing far too fast and I wanted desperately to slow it down and make it last.

We spent one week at home before leaving for Colorado on our honeymoon. We landed in Denver, rented a car, and were on our own schedule for a week. We did or didn't do whatever we wanted for seven blissful days. We've found we truly enjoy this type of travel. No schedules, no expectations.

Bob is a caring, loving husband who would never blurt out an unkind word in a heated moment. I, on the other hand, am often found apologizing for words that shouldn't have been spoken. We have improved our communications skills greatly since 1989. I believe this is key for any functional relationship, marital or otherwise. Bob is great at surprises. He'll plan an overnight away or deliver flowers for no reason.

Bob is a wonderful father. He brings lots of laughter and song to our home. Although he has not changed many diapers, he has taken the girls on many-a-jaunt out in the woods or to pet the baby animals at Ironwood's mini-farm. Sometimes he can't even find a pair of shoes sitting in front of him, but he gives us opportunities and experiences that few people have.

Our differences are great, but we focus on the positives each of us have to offer, and that makes for a grand marriage. Life has changed significantly for us in the past four years. Hannah didn't slow us down too much. She traveled with us every place we went. When Hannah was born I took four months off from IBM and then went back half-time. When Hannah turned two, I had to choose between going back to IBM full-time or leaving the company. We felt it best that I be home full-time rather than furthering a demanding career. Within five months we found out I was expecting triplets. In the meantime, I had opened a small antique and handiwork shop.

The birth of the triplets has slowed but not stopped us. I've recently completed my elementary education degree and plan on pursuing a teaching position when the girls are in school. I'm confident that, for now, God wants me at home enjoying our four beautiful girls.

We have purchased a large quilting machine that I use to hire-out machine quilting. Quilting has been a great refuge for me. My mother taught me to quilt when I was fifteen and I find this to be a great outlet for my creativity and a wonderful way to relax. I feel it's vital to pass on pieces of our heritage and ourselves. I treasure the quilts my mother made for me and hope my girls will cherish what I make for them. They are a reflection of my life, merged with Bob's and enhanced by the girls – each of a piece of God's handiwork woven together as the pieces of the quilt.

13

ATTITUDE OF GRATITUDE

"The greatest handicap I have now, is the
same one I had before my accident."

—Bob Bardwell

This simply means that my greatest handicap is from the
neck up. It's the attitudes we choose that control our lives. Our
greatest handicaps are negative attitudes we foster and nurture
in our hearts and minds until they cripple our lives. I say, "If
you're paralyzed from the neck up, you need a check up." Some
of our greatest handicaps include apathy, a bitter spirit and cares
of the world.

APATHY

Apathy is that complacent, lethargic attitude that says, "I
don't care." It's one thing to say, "I quit", "It doesn't work", or
"I've tried it before", but when you entertain the attitude, "I
don't care", it seems that all hope is gone. How often do you
find yourself in an environment where the attitude of those
around you is complacent?

I strongly believe that many good, well-
meaning people have fallen victim to compla-
cency. If you, as the reader, find yourself saying,
"I don't care," I encourage you to seek some
wise counsel and change that disabling attitude
to "I can" or "I did it."

BITTER SPIRIT

A bitter spirit, in my opinion, does more destruction to the life of a man than any other negative attitude. Bitterness seems to tear the fabric of the human spirit and leave a trail of anger, depression, and unforgiveness; all of which lead a person to misery and despair.

How is your spirit when you're ridiculed, falsely accused, or someone of less stature comes along and tries to correct you? How is your spirit when everything seems to be going great for the next person, and your life at the moment is in shambles?

Is your life slowly dying? Does everything you hoped for and dreamed of seem to be gone? Is your relationship with a friend or your spouse filled with brokenness, unforgiveness, resentment, and hatred?

BITTERNESS is probably the cause! I encourage you to turn to God, who offers strength for you to forgive, or to be forgiven.

CARES OF THE WORLD

This is the third of man's greatest handicaps. This one is easy to fall into and can be done by just getting too busy. Even though every activity in your schedule may be benevolent or intended for good, maybe you have gotten too busy for your spouse, children, neighbor, and God – priorities that have somehow been misplaced.

Matthew 13:22 says, *"...the worries of this life and the deceitfulness of wealth choke it (the good seed), making it unfruitful."*

Do your family and God get your leftover time? Is your attitude, "If there's time in my schedule, I'll have a family outing and/or attend church?" Your priorities tell a whole lot about your character.

Are the cares of the world crowding in your life and choking the real purpose in living? Like me, these things can slowly creep up on you and before you know it, you're caught in a trap.

Attitude has been called the "magic word." Chuck Swindoll says,

> "The longer I live, the more I realize the impact of attitude on life. Attitude, to me, is more important than the past, than education, than money, than circumstances, than failure, than successes, than what other people think or say or do. It is more important than appearance, giftedness or skill. It will make or break a company, a church, a home. The remarkable thing is we have a choice every day regarding the attitude we will embrace for that day. We cannot change our past . . .we cannot change the fact that people will act in a certain way. We cannot change the inevitable. The only thing we can do is play on the one thing we have and that is our attitude. I am convinced that life is 10% what happens to me and 90% how I react to it. And so it is with you."*

Wow, I like that definition. It tells me that no one but myself can give me a bad day.

> Like my 85-year-old neighbor Homer says, "I never have a bad day, just some better than others."

I can choose to blame Ray Richardson (who dropped the Caterpillar bucket on me) for ruining my life and all my goals and dreams. Or, I can choose to be the most blessed man on the face of the earth, and be grateful that I can still *"celebrate life."*

No Hint of Handicap

Clumping along the beach towards the water, I noticed how deeply my crutches were burrowing at each step, making progress a challenge.

*Used with permission by "Word Publishers," Dallas Texas.

Carefully keeping sand out of an open-toed cast, I was in a dark mood that contrasted the day's brightness.

I spotted a lone seagull eyeing me with interest. Then, scarcely believeing my eyes, I saw it. The bird, too, was dragging a useless leg. Of all the gulls, the one that took a liking to me was a fellow sufferer. Sharing lunch together, the bird and I developed a dialogue.

How difficult a bad leg must be in a seagull's competitive world. Yet its fat body, its feathers and the gleam in its eye revealed its secret.

Effortlessly soaring above the sand, it lost any hint of handicap. It was not limited by that useless leg, it could rise above it. The lesson was clear: I could choose to allow this condition to drag me down, or drawing upon God's resources, I could rise above it.

—Edward McRae

The ATTITUDE OF GRATITUDE

Can you think of any social graces which are more rare in our society than gratitude?

Children today are not being raised in a society that promotes and instills a spirit of gratitude. Being thankful for what we have and counting our blessings is just not cool. Looking on the good side of things and saying only a "good word" about others is very rare behavior. As I travel and visit schools, service clubs, hospitals, churches, and give speeches at banquets, rallies, sports events, etc., I see a noticeable lack of gratitude.

WHAT WERE MY PROBLEMS AGAIN?

I regularly get calls from the Mayo Clinic hospital asking me to visit someone who was just injured and is in intensive care with a spinal cord injury. I go and try to cheer them up, because after all, I went through the same rehabilitation they are going through. After introducing myself and chatting for a brief time, I assure them I will return. You know what happens nearly every time I leave the room? I go out scratching my head saying to myself, "What were my problems again?"

Did my problems go away? Of course not. I got my mind off myself and met face-to-face with someone in much more pain— maybe someone who is young or has a much greater injury level, not able to wiggle a finger, or someone wearing a "halo" on their head. I can no longer even begin to think the old pity line, "No one has it quite as rough as me."

ATTITUDE DETERMINES ALTITUDE

How's your attitude right now? Maybe it's time for a trip to the hospital, to a neighbor, or down the street to help someone less fortunate than yourself. Just maybe you will find something for which to be grateful! Just in case nothing pops into your head, here is a starter:

1) Can you see the magic of a leaf, a butterfly, a snowflake, an eagle, or a rainbow?

2) Did you know that every time you hear a robin sing, the wind blowing, or the words "I love you," 24,000 fibers are vibrating in your ear?

3) 500 muscles move every time you walk, run, dance, work or play.

4) Steel and metal tarnish and rust with wear, but your skin is constantly renewing itself.

"HEY CHUM, MY BUM'S NUMB!"

For 16 years I had eluded major pressure sore problems on my *"back porch"*. Because I knew the consequences of breaking down tissue, I always would use expensive cushions to sit on. When paralyzed from the waist down, there's very little butt muscle left (believe me), so it's important to protect the tissue. For tissue to be healthy, it needs plenty of air, light, and movement, but when you can't walk, stand, or fly, what options does a person have? After extensive travel and not taking care of myself, reality finally caught up with me and I had to face the music and have surgery.

January 1989

It all began, on the 1st, New Years day,
When family came over for fun and pictionary to play.

But on the 3rd, I packed up my bags and took a ride,
It's off to St. Mary's hospital, safely to abide.

The reason, quite simply, it was the bum,
With surgery in sight, I'm glad it was numb.

With Black and Decker and all the other fancy tools,
I stayed awake, so the doctors would keep all the rules.

With bone chipped away, and the sutchers sewn up tight,
Dr. Kay says it went fine, but the right cheek is really a sight.

It's off to my room, all tucked in 2-143,
Push the button, ESPN I get to see!

Nurse pops in, your back porch can I see,
For four straight weeks, the most popular sight to see.

Then it happens, at 5:30 a.m., she pops on the light,
Mr. Bardwell, you never went to the bathroom last night.

You must go to the bathroom, your jug I will bring,
Nurse, be gone, be gone or your neck I will wring.

Family and friends stop in and bring lots of delight,
their smiles, kind words and cheer are a most welcome sight.

One special friend with card and flowers she came,
Jode, yes, I know, I know that was her name.

Infection, infection, it struck right in the butt,
Doctor takes a look and all the sutchers he does cut.

It's back to square one, with IV, high temperature and pain,
I know, it's the needles, hard times and trouble that bring
  gain.

It's down to the whirlpool, in the dunk tank twice a day,
So relaxing and warm, please Betty, ten more minutes can I
  stay?

I must ask the Doctor, and have him think it was he,
who thought of letting me go home early and just let me be.

I finally made it and quite a month it has been indeed,
Now, a bit more healing, strength, & shower is all I need.

HOME, SWEET, HOME!

I got home, and for the next three to four weeks, I had to lay on my stomach. I put a mattress on the floor and was able to do typing and office work off the end of the mattress. One day I dragged myself over to the mattress and looked down in dismay. I had two rug burns on each knee about two inches in size. They were raw and now I could no longer lay on my stomach because I had to bandage my knees. My only choice left, was to lay on my side.

I propped up a pillow against my back, and held my head up a bit to do my office work. This all went well for about two days, until my neck started to hurt. I had gotten an enlarged nerve in my neck from leaning on it. I think this was Murphy's law in action.

Well, things *did* improve. I guess they couldn't have gotten much worse. How was my ATTITUDE? Yes, I struggled a lot, but I didn't become bitter. I followed the wise proverb from the Old Testament, Proverbs 17:22: *"A cheerful heart is a good medicine."* I'm a firm believer in the "healing power of a healthy mind." The mind is connected to every cell and system in the body, and it's good health or lack of it affects the healing process. I was determined to make the best of it and give thanks that things weren't any worse. Finally, the healing came.

14

TWENTY-YEAR DREAM COME TRUE

"If God is in your dream, no request is too extreme"
—Copied

The purpose of this chapter is to encourage those who are still dreaming and wondering and thinking your dreams have been forgotten. I want you to know that some of our greatest treasures take a lot more patience and time than we think we have.

I don't consider myself a 'dreamer', but I know we all have some dreams, secret or expressed, that we hope will come true.

On July 16, 1973, as a result of my injury, I was told that I could not become the biological father of a child. This fact was very painful, but I kept it inside. I felt cheated and wondered if this reality could ever be changed. Accepting the fact that I would be in a wheelchair the rest of my life was a reality I felt I could adjust to and face its challenges. Not being able to become a father was tough mentally. I wrestled with this greatly.

Jode and I contacted two different adoption agencies, and at the same time I was constantly quizzing my doctors at the Mayo Clinic about some new technology to make this happen. As far as I knew for all these years, I did not even have a live sperm cell. When you're paralyzed from the belly button down, nothing below that functions normally.

Down deep in my heart, I felt somehow, in some way, God

would intervene and bring a child into my life.

Shortly after Jode and I were married in 1991, I pushed on the door at the clinic a bit harder and made an appointment with the fertility department. After several visits and phone calls we were told that some new technology would soon be available for us to try. The day finally arrived when the call came from Dr. Lewis for us to come to the clinic.

A 1% CHANCE IS 100% BETTER THAN ZERO!

The first four months of going through this procedure was disheartening, but we had confidence and faith that whatever was the end result was God's will.

The scenario:

Very expensive; five months in duration; one-to-two percent chance; no guarantees. The five month limitation was because of the possible risks involved to go any further.

We went into the fifth month thinking God must have Plan B waiting for us. Jode was taking fertility drugs that I had to administer via shots twice daily. Just the thought of needles turns my stomach. I do not like to get poked with a needle. Call me a wimp, I don't care. Being the needle had to be given in the 'back porch,' I thought I could attach the needle to a wall some way and Jode could just put the caboose in reverse and the connection could be made without me seeing it.

Well, I did learn to do the needle trick and somehow during this fifth month we had messed up on the correct dosage. Besides the overdose, the insemination was delayed. We were glad it was soon to be over and we could go on with our lives and see what God might have for us next.

Going back for that ultrasound a few weeks later was the ultimate in celebration. I know I stood up and ran around the room when I saw our child's heartbeat!

OUR MIRACLE BABY!

Twenty years ago from my injury I was told,
a child of yours to conceive, you will never hold.
I was so sad and disappointed, but accepted my plight,
Oh, DEAR LORD, I prayed, isn't there a glimmer of light?
Well, the many years passed and waiting I was still,
but a call came from Mayo Clinic, oh what a thrill.
Would you like to be the man to give our new program a
   test?
Bring your wife Jode, and we'll do our very best.
Yes, Dr. Lewis, tell us when and look no more,
We're looking forward to the challenge, meet you on the
   fourth floor.
With a 1% chance for five months repeat,
We look at the ultrasound, and there is a miracle heartbeat.
For nine months we wait to CELEBRATE this gift more
   precious than gold,
On February 1, 1993, Hannah Rose, an 8 pound 4 ounce
   beautiful girl we hold.

How did I feel? Wheelchair, no legs needed, flying.
                                        —Bob Bardwell

The miracle birth story of Hannah Rose was on television
that night and articles were in several newspapers the next few
days.

I wondered, if God knew that Jode was going to become
pregnant in the fifth and last month, why didn't He have it happen the first month? Think of the mental and emotional strain
we could have saved, not to mention several thousand dollars
we could have given to charity! I wasn't complaining, just
being human in questioning.

I knew God has a reason for everything and His timing is
always perfect. The nine months passed and it was Superbowl
Sunday January 31, 1993. Jode woke me at midnight and off to
the hospital we went.

The next day, February 1, at 3:11 in the afternoon, a beautiful 8 pound 4 ounce baby girl was in my arms. I gave a celebration cheer when she kicked her legs. I thought she might be born a paraplegic (ha). A few days after we brought her home, I received a call from Marion Richardson, the wife of Ray (the man who had dropped the caterpillar bucket on me 19 years earlier). She said she had something to tell me that I didn't know. I drove to her home. She came out and brought along the article from the paper. She was very emotional and excited when she said that Hannah Rose was born on Ray's birthday. Ray died of diabetes a few years earlier. We cried tears of joy together and realized now why we got pregnant in the fifth month. God had a plan with a special blessing.

Hannah ("ha ha", as she says) is four years old now and has given me the most wonderful four years of my life. One of the most rewarding experiences for a parent is to see your child experience things for the first time. She gets so excited and claps her hands over the simplest things.

Yes, 20 years of waiting seems like a moment now that we have Hannah. I'm reminded of what the Psalmist David said in Psalm 37:4 *"Delight yourself in the Lord and he will give you the desires of your heart."*

> Dear Bob & family,
>
> We saw you and your family on the news a few weeks ago. It was nice to see some positive news for a change. Our congratulations to you on the birth of Hannah! Her name was our choice for a girl, but we were given four boys.
>
> We hope to meet Hannah in the future.
>
> Grace and Love,
>
> Jim & Laurie Busch

To you who are still waiting for that dream, I understand the anxiety and frustration. But waiting, as difficult as it is, produces in us a trust and reliance on God that comes no other way.

Soon after Hannah was born, Jode and I hoped that maybe God had a brother or sister for Hannah to play with. We returned to the Mayo Clinic for one more chance to have a child. We started in August of 1993 and Dr. Lewis had given us eight months for this try. Things were just not lining up and it looked like another child was not to be. After several missed months and failed attempts, it was December of 1994, our last month again.

We returned in January for an ultrasound. I was sitting waiting anxiously for some news. The doctor walked into the room and said, "Bob, it's a good thing you are sitting down." I replied: "Well, doctor, I haven't had a problem with standing up the past 21 years."

"Bob and Jode," she said, "you aren't having one baby; you aren't having two babies; you are having three babies." I was speechless for a few seconds and said, "Thank you, God," then returned to a state of mild, but good, shock.

In Ephesians 3:20, the Apostle Paul speaks of God as, " . . . *him who is able to do immeasurably more than all we ask or imagine. . . "*

This news was a bit overwhelming, but we both went home rejoicing as well as discussing some of the changes that would be necessary.

MIRACLES NEVER CEASE

For the past 2 and a half years, our miracle baby "Hannah"
    has been a real delight,
So why not ask God for another child and try again, right?
So we started the procedure at Mayo's Fertility Clinic on the
    fourth floor,
But things didn't look too hopeful each time we
    walked/rolled out the door.
With months quickly passing and insurance soon to end,
It looked as though this time around a child the Lord would
    choose not to send.

We returned in January to have our last ultrasound, you see,
the doctor said, **"Congratulations, Congratulations,
Congratulations;** not 1, not 2, but 3."

Someone reminded me of the famous words, "It's not over
until it's over,"

For us it was the bottom of the 9th, 2 outs, and we got a
three-run homer!

The night before they were born, Jode, Hannah and I were at
the local county fair,

You wouldn't believe the people who would stop, turn, and
stare!

By 1:00 p.m. on August 2nd, three healthy beautiful girls I
was blessed to hold.

Yes, many of the gifts from the Lord are truly more precious
than gold.

We had names for triplets like Lucy, Lynn, and Lolly, or
Larry, Curley, and Moe,

But really it's Lydia Jean, Elizabeth Birdie and Abigail Jo.

Yes, I'm outnumbered 5 to 1 but Hannah has three siblings
with which she can play.

So for now it's 20 diapers, a gallon of milk, washing, crying,
burping and chaos all in a day.

———————————————

The nine months went quickly (at least for me) and Jode's
pregnancy went extremely well. We had joined the "Triplet
Connection," a non-profit agency in California as a resource for
networking, etc. We bought a van (extended model), ordered a
triplet stroller, and rounded up three cribs. Not knowing their
sexes until birth, you wouldn't believe the clothes we had collected.

We received from approximately 30 companies everything
from toys to baby spoons. A friend worked for a food brokerage
company and collected diapers which needed to be taken off the
shelves due to a packaging change. We had several hundred
packages piled to the ceiling of our extra bathroom.

Finally the exciting day came at 36 weeks to go to the hospital and have the C-section surgery to deliver the babies.

ITS A GIRL, ITS A GIRL, ITS A GIRL!

We got to the hospital at 7 a.m. and were in the delivery room ready to go at noon. Jode was all prepped and I was close by with a towel to pull over my head if I couldn't handle the surgery.

Within a span of about two minutes, out they came weighing in at 4 lb. 10 oz, 5 lb. 5 oz. and 6 lb. 1 oz. Whopping babies for triplets! The doctor said, "It's a girl, it's a girl, it's a girl."

I was hoping for at least one boy to carry on my wrestling legacy and provide a body guard for his sisters later on. But we rejoiced in what God had given us. Three healthy and beautiful girls. We had bought Hannah three dollies to prepare her for the coming intrusion in her life. The day came and I brought her to the hospital to see her sisters.

She was 2-1/2, so she stood on a stool, to meet her sisters. You should have seen her eyes as she reached out and touched each one. They all came home after seven days in the hospital, and the adventure was soon to begin.

Yes, it has been an adventure for about two years and things are changing each day. We haven't done it alone. We have been extremely blessed with many different close friends to help care for the girls. (Melisa Brandt, Teri Laschkewitsch, Jenny and Jackie Peterson, Elaine Froiland, Carol Raygor, Carol Wyland, Connie McKenzie and several others.)

> I can handle the girls for about 30 minutes and then run out of options as they are all screaming for their mom. If Jode is not home when she says she will be, I call 911.

It's a challenge now and I know it will get greater, but we take it one day at a time and strive to be the best parents these girls could have. I'll tell you how we have done when they have their triple wedding.

P.S. — We have informed the Mayo Clinic that we will not be returning again!

15

JOY IN THE JOURNEY

"For when I am weak, then I am strong."
—2 Cor. 12:10

Its early March of 1997 and I'm writing this last chapter from Gulf Shores, Alabama. I'm looking out at the waves on the gulf from the fifth floor of my father-in-law's condo. We loaded up our Dodge Caravan (extended) with the four girls, a friend, Jackie, clothes for the week, triplet stroller, wheelchair, safety seats, and three portable cribs, and drove 1,300 miles. We would have made a great ad for the Chrysler Corporation!

There has been lots of joy in my journey, as has been obvious from the preceding chapters. That doesn't mean that I or my family have been exempt from life's bumps, bruises, flat tires, and headaches. It means we have an inner joy that has seen us through the storms.

In this last chapter I would like to share some of the bits and pieces of what's going on in my life, what's important to me, and leave you with some reminders and final thoughts.

ONE DAY AT A TIME

Living by this concept is one of the best remedies for mental health. One of the questions that children ask me is, "You mean you will be in a wheelchair the rest of your life?" I explain, "Yes, as far as I know, but you know what? I take it one day at a time." The rest of my life is hopefully a long time, but I have reason to get up today, a purpose to live, and something significant to do. If tomorrow comes, I will do it all over again and celebrate each day that I'm given.

Yes, I'll make some mistakes and wrong decisions, but I have found they too can often have a positive ending. I'm reminded of the story in Texas of the little girl named Jessica who fell in a well. As the well was being built, the well drillers hit a hard ledge of rock, causing the well to drift. This was not corrected, but left imperfect. Who would have ever guessed that this imperfection would later save the life of this child who fell in the well but got caught on the ledge?

My accident has elevated my awareness of being grateful for each sunrise and sunset. Because of my priorities, what was important to me yesterday, may have to "fall through the cracks" today.

Who is in charge of your day? We like to think "I am." But in reality it's often our neighbor, boss, spouse, or friend that disappoints us and dampens our day. I challenge you to put God in charge of your day, making human disappointments not as significant.

If you want to live each day to the fullest, my recommendation is:
1) Be unafraid of change;
2) Be interested in big things;
3) Be happy in small ways;
4) Give God the glory.

One Day at a Time

One day at a time, sweet Jesus, that is all I'm asking from you, just give me the strength to do every day what I gotta' do. Yesterday's gone, sweet Jesus, and tomorrow may never be mine, so for my sake teach me to take, ONE DAY AT A TIME.

*Kris Kristofferson and Marijohn Wilkin

*Used with permission by "Buckhorn Music Publishers, Inc." © 1973

BLOOM WHERE YOU ARE PLANTED

So often in my counseling, people seem to struggle with where God wants them, and they continually wonder if they are in God's will. My first response is, "God probably wants you right where you are for the time being. The question is, "Are you doing your best and putting your whole heart into it?" In other words, "Are you blooming where you have been planted?"

Concentrate and focus on what you have in front of you. Being faithful and diligent in what you are doing often leads to change and other greater challenges.

The happiest people on earth are not people without problems and trials, but rather they are the people who have accepted them and are striving to bloom where they have been planted.

TRIPLETS - A THREE-RING CIRCUS

A three-ring circus is an accurate description of our home — at least for now. Having triplet girls who are almost two and a four-year old girl definitely challenges time-management skills. The lyric to the song by Debbie Boone, "Just when you get it all worked out, that's when the changes come," is standard operating procedure at our home. Jode and I have found that setting and following our priorities each day is the key to good time-management. Once you decide what is important in your life, you can go through the day knowing you will have unfinished business but will have accomplished the most important things. God and family are top priorities for us. Jode and I strive to invest our time, treasures, and talents so that the most is being accomplished toward what God wants us to do.

THREE REASONS PEOPLE DON'T HAVE TIME:
1) They are doing the wrong thing.
2) They are doing too much.
3) They are doing things the wrong way.

The camp, wheelchair sports, book writing, counseling and speaking are all important — but not the most important. You can start, fail, and start over again and be successful in business, but not in child raising. God has given us the present to raise them with a balance of love and discipline, and in a few blinks they are grown and gone.

PRECIOUS MOMENTS

1) When the triplets were six months old, Hannah was three. I came in the house and there was Jode sitting on the floor, bottle feeding one baby in her arm and bottle feeding another one laying on the floor. The third baby was sleeping nearby and Hannah was sitting in front, flipping pages of a book that mom was reading. How resourceful! I never thought of doing it that way!

2) Having the girls take turns standing on my feet giving them wheelie rides in my wheelchair.

3) Hannah said the one day, "Dad, you need four legs" as they were all trying to climb on my lap.

4) Just as I was writing this, Hannah called up to me from the swimming pool, "Dad, look I'm swimming all by myself."

5) Watching them play 'Ring Around The Rosey' with Hannah, the "all fall down" part is hilarious!

6) Reminding them as they all carry four week old kittens, not to carry them by the neck or tail, for fear they may become paraplegics!

A friend reminded me, "Bob, there is joy in your journey now, but I'll check in with you when the triplets all turn sixteen." No, it's not easy having three crying children at your side, a four-year old wanting your attention, meals to prepare, diapers to change, laundry to do (I matched (tried to) and folded 52 pairs of socks one night), house to clean, bills to pay, doors and drawers to kidproof . . . the list never ends!

In addition, Jode does quilting and has an antique shop. We just recently found that if each triplet knows one-third of how to do something, we should consider it done. We, like you, have a lot to juggle, but communication along with organization, and knowing each day what's most important, sure does help.

LOG HOME

We live in a beautiful log home, built in 1983, next to Ironwood. I had lived in a mobile home from 1973-1983. My workman's compensation company called me and asked if they could stop by for a visit. They said, "Bob, it's the 10-year anniversary of your accident, and you have been a model client for us. It's the 75th anniversary for our company, so we have decided to build you a new house. Take six months to decide what you want and we will start the construction."

Wow! Just how often does a workman's compensation company decide to build a nice log home for someone, just because of an anniversary? I took the six months to design and make plans for the log home and thought, just in case God blesses me with children someday, I better put in a few extra bedrooms. Well, they sat empty for 10 years and now I could use an another one! I have been blessed to be covered by a cooperative company who cares for my well-being. (They have also provided an all-terrain vehicle (ATV) for me to get around in at the camp.)

1996 HUNTING SEASON (BEST EVER)

Turkey! May 1st: I was sitting in a turkey blind about two miles from my house with my good friend Joel Raygor. It was 5:30 a.m. Not even the birds were awake yet, let alone me. I was quietly getting last-minute instructions for when this big Tom Turkey would arrive. At 7:04 out struts a Jake (young male) at our decoy. At 7:05 I bagged my first Tom Turkey!

Geese! October 15th: I was sitting in an underground, heated, camouflaged blind hunting Canada geese. We were in the middle of a picked cornfield just outside Rochester. A professional guide service company in Rochester volunteered to take me and see how it would go for someone with a disability. The procedure: The guide called the geese in with his little 'honking' device, plus put out plenty of decoys. When the guide saw geese approaching, he pushed a button and a little red light came on in front of me. That means 'get ready!' When the buzzer went off, the door above me slid open and I was supposed to *stand up* and shoot. On my first try, I had two problems:

1) My head got caught in the door as it was opening. Guides went bananas!

2) I could not stand up, so all I could see was blue sky.

Before the next flock came in, we rearranged my seating. I managed to keep my head out of the door, and I bagged two nice honkers. I thanked the guys for the adventure, we had a few good laughs, and I headed for home with my hunting story.

White Tail Deer! November 11th: It was the last day of whitetail deer hunting. I was sitting out in the woods in my El Camino with my 20-gauge shotgun at my side. Seemingly from out of nowhere, a buck came walking toward me. He kept coming. I didn't know it at the time, but he was handicapped and no doubt saw my handicapped license plate and thought this guy can't do much harm.

Well, he turned and walked off into the woods just in line with my gun barrel. I bagged him. Yes, he had a front club foot and a broken antler. Sure did make for some good venison!

1996 PARALYMPICS IN ATLANTA

In April I got a call from Joni Erickson Tada wondering if I would be interested in going to Atlanta in August to be a chaplain at the Paralympics. Many of you may recognize Joni, a quadriplegic resulting from a diving accident. She has a non-profit Christian agency called "Joni and Friends" in California, which ministers around the world to the disabled community, as well as making society aware of the many ways they can be involved in encouraging those with disabilities. Joni impacted my life early in my injury by her book and movie called, "Joni." Her life and message of hope and faith in the Lord continues to change lives. The Paralympics followed the regular Olympics in Atlanta and used the same facilities. There were 4,000 disabled athletes from over 100 countries, competing in 75 different events.

I spent ten fantastic days as a chaplain and coach sharing the good news of Jesus Christ by way of handing out literature and a pin which said, "More than Gold." Each day was also mixed with talking, praying, and encouraging the athletes. I watched and videotaped many of the track and field events because I knew many of the athletes personally.

> I came away from the Paralympics with a new motto for sports, "The older I get, the better I was!"

I keep in mind this motto as I continue racing toward my goal of 100 marathons. I no longer do 72-mile training runs, however, I do a bit of training on Wednesday nights with racing buddies Tony Possehl, Maynard Read, Mike Kuhlmann, and Brian Betlach. My only other training is trying to keep up with four daughters.

MOTIVATIONAL SPEAKING:

I have enjoyed doing motivational speaking more than 300 times at the local and national level the past 12 years. I've been a keynote speaker at schools, sporting events, camps, special banquets, teacher's workshops, corporate businesses such as IBM, churches, and other community functions. My life and message has something for everyone. I am cutting back my speaking now with my family, but look forward to every opportunity I am able to take.

> During one of my elementary school assemblies, I was telling the students that I can do almost anything as long as I have some adaptive equipment and a helping hand. A first grader raised his hand and asked, "How do you play kickball?" Smart kid!

Being an inspirational/motivational speaker is a wonderful challenge. I try always to live what I am striving to motivate others to do.

24 YEARS OF LIFE IN A WHEELCHAIR

Yes, it's still frustrating and inconvenient. Some days I would like to throw the chair over the riverbank, but I have found that getting it back is a lot of work. Two nasty 'P's' are constant challenges I seem to face each day: plumbing and pressure sores.

Keeping healthy kidneys, bladder, and other digestive organs is vital to my health. Infection seems to be always lurking, making diet and liquid very important. I have severe burning and stinging continually in my right hip. At times it gets nearly intolerable, but I put my mind on something else, or get busy, and that seems to help. I have tried drugs and different types of therapy, but for now it's something I have to learn to live with.

There is almost always another side to pain— if you look for it. The joys, experiences, and opportunities of being a paraplegic have far outweighed the challenges. I used to say, "Why me?" now I say, "Why not me?"

Counting my different chairs and vehicles, I have 68 wheels instead of two legs, and wheels are much faster than legs. I pull up to the front door of the shopping mall because of the handicap parking sign and once my wheels hit the hard surface my shopping is short lived.

Instead of being 5-feet-9, I am 4-feet tall. How tall are kids? Just my height! We talk eye-to-eye and I can easily put my arm around them, which makes for real special times. I know I have been able to touch the lives of many youth and adults as a result of my injury.

When I think of how each of us can make a difference I think of the starfish story. Someone was walking along the beach and came upon millions of starfish that had been washed up on the land as a result of the lower tide. He took them one by one and ran to the sea and threw them back. Someone else came along and said, "Sir, don't you think you are wasting your time with the millions of starfish?" He answered, "No, I made a difference in that one."

I have been sent hundreds of letters like this one: "Whenever my situation gets to me, you come to mind. Many times in the privacy of your mind, you must long to be free of your disability. Thank you for allowing the Lord to use your disability to make some of my 'struggling moments' easier." -Noel

---

I also remember that "Sometimes the Lord calms the storm; sometimes He lets the storm rage and calms the child."

THE JOURNEY CONTINUES . . .

I would guess if I write another book, it might be on raising kids, finishing 100 marathons, and other ventures. Some of you will want to know how Hannah and the triplets turned out. I trust the stories I have told, experiences that I have shared, and the message I have spoken from my heart has provided hope, encouragement, humor, and healing in your life's journey.

I also have a vision that if the publishing of this book turns out to be successful, I would like to see it made into a video or a movie called "Wheels of Fire."

When you're struggling, remember this acronym:

J-Jesus O-Others Y-You.

Joy put in this order will ensure more JOY in your journey!

TRIBULATIONS

Looking back it seems to me
all the pain which had to be,
left me when the pain was ov'r
richer than I'd been before.

And by every hurt and blow
suffered in the long ago,
I can face the world today
in a bigger, kinder way.

Pleasure doesn't make a man
life requires a sterner plan,
for he who never knows a care
never knows what he can bear.

— Anonymous

GOD'S PLAN OF SALVATION

1. **Recognize yourself as a sinner.**
   Romans 3:23 *"for all have sinned and fell short of the glory of God"*
   Jeremiah 17:9 *"The heart is deceitful about all things and beyond cure. Who can understand it."*

2. **Acknowledge you can't save yourself.**
   Titus 3:5 *"He saved us, not because of righteous things we have done but because of his mercy."*
   Mark 8:36 *"What good is it for a man to gain the whole world, yet forfeit his soul?"*

3. **Believe and Receive God's gift of his Son as payment for your sins.**
   Ephesians 2:8-9 *"For it is by grace you have been saved through faith and this not from yourselves, it is the gift of God - not by works, so that no one can boast."*
   Romans 6:23 *"for the wages of sin is death, but the gift of God is eternal life in Christ Jesus our Lord."*
   Romans 10:13 *"Everyone who calls on the name of the Lord will be saved."*

Religion is man through his efforts striving to get to Heaven. Christianity is a personal relationship with Jesus Christ as Lord and Savior.

Are you a professor or a possessor?

MOTIVATIONAL SPEAKING INFO

What other motivators talk about, Bob lives...
that's the difference.

Organizations... *"Selecting Bob to be the keynote speaker at your special event is a **fantastic** choice. Bob and I were injured the same year, 1973, and having a close friendship with him has been both supportive and very inspiring.*
—Karl Kassulke, *Minnesota Viking defense for 12 years*
Eagan, Minnesota

Colleges... *"Huntington College had the priviledge to host Mr. Bardwell at a student assembly. Bob was an **outstanding speaker** as he captured the hearts of our student body. He communicated in a way that students really connected with – and they were 'charged' with his inspiration and energy. He is a very motivational presenter.* —Huntington College
Huntington, Indiana

Churches... *"I have known Bob since college days and have watched his faith and love for Christ challenged through his trials. He will impact every listener in your church by his life and message.*
—Pastor Larry Forsberg, *Oakridge Community Church*
Stillwater, Minnesota

Businesses... *"Having Bob in our area serving as a **positive role model** and friend is a real plus to our community. He is an active speaker at our schools, churches, businesses and community events. His name is frequently seen at the local, county and state level. Businesses such as IBM and Mayo Clinic have benefited greatly from his talks.*
—Mayor Chuck Hazama, Rochester, Minnesota

Schools... *"I've worked with Bob in a school setting for over 10 years and can tell you from experience that there's something **captivating** about Bob's life, story, and humor. Bob's perseverance, positive attitude and motivation make him a great role model for kids. **Bob's the one.***
—Joe Stanich, Rochester Public Schools
Rochester, Minnesota

ORDER FORM

Please send me _____ copy (copies) of *The Marathons of Life* by Bob Bardwell, at a cost of $12.95 each. Include a $2.00 shipping and handling cost for a total of $14.95. In Minnesota, add 6.5% sales tax for a total of $15.79 per book.

☐ Check enclosed for _____

☐ Bill my credit card (Visa or Mastercard)

Card Number: _____

Expiration Date: _____

Signature: _____

Date: _____

Name _____

Company _____

Address _____

City _____

State _____ Zip_____

☐ Yes, I would like the book(s) autographed to:

_____

_____

_____

_____

Mail to: Bob Bardwell
            7291 CR 6 SW
            Stewartville, MN 55976
            Phone: (507) 533-9516
            Toll Free: 1-888-598-4300